Thunder in the Soul

Thunder in the Soul

To Be Known by God

Abraham Joshua Heschel

Edited by Robert Erlewine

PLOUGH PUBLISHING HOUSE

Published by Plough Publishing House
Walden, New York
Robertsbridge, England
Elsmore, Australia
www.plough.com

Cover art copyright © 2021 by Julie Lonneman.

Reprinted by permission of Farrar, Straus and Giroux:

Excerpts from *God in Search of Man* by Abraham Joshua Heschel. Copyright © 1955 by Abraham Joshua Heschel. Copyright renewed 1983 by Sylvia Heschel.

Excerpts from *The Insecurity of Freedom* by Abraham Joshua Heschel. Copyright © 1966 by Abraham Joshua Heschel. Copyright renewed 1994 by Sylvia Heschel.

Excerpts from *Man Is Not Alone* by Abraham Joshua Heschel. Copyright © 1951 by Abraham J. Heschel. Copyright renewed 1979 by Sylvia Heschel.

Excerpts from *The Sabbath* by Abraham Joshua Heschel. Copyright © 1951 by Abraham Joshua Heschel. Copyright renewed 1979 by Sylvia Heschel.

Reprinted by permission of Farrar, Straus and Giroux on behalf of the Heschel Estate:

Excerpts from *Man's Quest for God* by Abraham Joshua Heschel. Copyright © 1954 by Abraham Joshua Heschel. Copyright renewed 1982 by Susannah Heschel and Sylvia Heschel.

Reprinted by permission of HarperCollins Publishers:

Excerpts from *The Prophets* by Abraham J. Heschel. Copyright © 1962 by Abraham J. Heschel.

A catalog record for this book is available from the British Library.
Library of Congress Cataloging-in-Publication Data

Names: Heschel, Abraham Joshua, 1907-1972, author. | Erlewine, Robert, editor.
Title: Thunder in the soul : to be known by God / Abraham Joshua Heschel ;
    edited by Robert Erlewine.
Description: Walden, New York : Plough Publishing House, [2020]
Identifiers: LCCN 2020041160 (print) | LCCN 2020041161 (ebook) | ISBN
    9780874863512 (paperback) | ISBN 9780874863529 (ebook)
Subjects: LCSH: God (Judaism)--Philosophy. | Jewish philosophy.
Classification: LCC BM610 .H482 2020 (print) | LCC BM610 (ebook) | DDC
    296.7--dc23
LC record available at https://lccn.loc.gov/2020041160
LC ebook record available at https://lccn.loc.gov/2020041161

Printed in the United States of America

Contents

Who Was Abraham Joshua Heschel?

Robert Erlewine

ABRAHAM JOSHUA HESCHEL is a singular figure in American Jewish history and modern Jewish thought. His life and work defy easy categorization, bringing together an array of seemingly contradictory tendencies. While rooted in traditionalist Judaism, he is attendant to the forces of modernity. A religiously observant Jew, he nevertheless insists that creative dissent is essential for the vitality of tradition. Fluent in Talmud, and deeply knowledgeable of traditional Jewish learning more generally, he is also at home in philosophy and modern biblical criticism. His most significant works address a popular audience, with prose accessible and often quite beautiful, and yet their premises are sophisticated and complex. Additionally, he is the rare modern Jewish thinker whose work reflects a profound knowledge of all genres of Jewish expression: Bible, Talmud, Midrash, medieval philosophy, Kabbalah, Hasidism, and modern thought. Even the language in which he composed his works varied; he wrote eloquent prose in four languages: Hebrew, German, English, and Yiddish.

Heschel offered a galvanizing vision of Judaism that was at times sharply critical of the status quo, while remaining deeply anchored in tradition. He rejected the notion that worship and religious practice were private matters, arguing instead that they have vital relevance for addressing the most pressing concerns of society. And he insisted this was the case even if it meant giving voice to views that were unpopular or controversial. Heschel's theological commitments undergirded his courageous efforts on behalf of the civil rights movement, his protests against the war in Vietnam, and his work to improve Jewish-Christian relations. Not adhering to any particular denomination of American Judaism, he engaged them all. He also maintained dialogue and friendships with leading Christian thinkers of his day.

Considering this vision and strength of character, it should not be surprising that nearly five decades after his death in 1972, he remains a towering figure in the consciousness of the American Jewish community and beyond. Indeed, his writings have had a global reach, with his books translated into many languages including Hebrew, Spanish, French, German, Croatian, Portuguese, Lithuanian, Urdu, Chinese, Korean, Japanese, Polish, and Dutch.

Heschel was born in Warsaw, Poland, in 1907. His lineage was illustrious, with many prominent rabbis on both sides of his family tree, including his namesake, the legendary Hasidic rebbe known as the Apter Rav, Avraham Yehoshua Heshel (1748–1825). As was the custom, he began studying Torah at three years of age and quickly showed himself to be a child prodigy. Significant energy and attention were devoted to his education in the traditional sources. Given his ancestry, upbringing, and intellectual abilities, he seemed destined to become a Hasidic rebbe.

And yet Heschel did not become a rebbe, at least not in a traditional sense. During his teenage years he developed an avid interest in literature and began writing poetry in Yiddish. With support from his mother (his father died during an epidemic in 1916), Heschel attended a secular Jewish gymnasium in Vilna for a year as preparation for university. While there, he was a member of Yung Vilna, a renowned Yiddish poetry group. In the fall of 1927, when he was twenty years old, he arrived in Berlin. At this time, Berlin was a major intellectual hub, not only of science, literature, art, and philosophy but also of Yiddish culture and the academic study of Judaism. He enrolled in the University of Berlin, where he studied philosophy, Semitics, and art history, and in the Hochschule für die Wissenschaft des Judentums, which trained liberal rabbis and scholars. He also studied at the Orthodox Hildesheimer rabbinical college, though he had already received Orthodox rabbinical ordination in Warsaw. Heschel showed a remarkable capacity to be at home in all Jewish communities, a trait that would be prominently displayed for the rest of his life.

He continued to write and publish poetry while finishing his dissertation, "Das prophetische Bewusstsein" (The Prophetic Consciousness), which he submitted in December 1932. The dissertation was subsequently published as a monograph, *Die Prophetie* (On Prophecy), in 1936. Almost three decades later, in 1962, an expanded English language translation, *The Prophets*, was published. On the surface, *Die Prophetie* is a work of comparative religion, in that it seeks to elucidate what makes the classical prophets of the Bible distinct as religious figures. While rooted in solid philological and historical scholarship, this work is, in fact, quite radical and subversive. It rejects the dominant tendencies in Protestant scholarship on the prophets, particularly the attempt to characterize the lives and visions of the prophets as evidence of mental illness, but also takes issue with the efforts of liberal Jewish interpreters to cast the prophets as rationalist philosophers. Instead, Heschel seeks to provide a more appropriate set of categories for understanding prophecy among the ancient Israelites. Thus, while this work employs the terminology and conventions of comparative religion as it was practiced at that time in Germany, it also calls attention to fundamental deficiencies of this discipline.

In addition to criticizing the methods used in the comparative study of religions, Heschel challenges the dominant assumptions of the philosophy and theology of his day. At its most profound level, *Die Prophetie* offers a meditation on, and critique of, the manner in which God and revelation have been understood in the West. In order to appreciate the prophets, Heschel insists, one must first clear away obstacles to understanding biblical thinking. First and foremost, this means rejecting philosophical views which render the idea of God's pathos – the inner, emotional life of God – unthinkable and even embarrassing. The biblical God is neither distant and impersonal like Aristotle's unmoved mover, nor an all-powerful lawgiver demanding obedience. Rather, with his notion of divine pathos, Heschel presents God as profoundly concerned with human behavior and history, and, indeed, as vulnerable, in a very real sense, to human affairs. Human actions affect God, bringing God grief, anger, or joy and strengthening or diminishing God's presence in the world. Far from an imperfection, this vulnerability defines God's relationship with human beings.

In 1937, Heschel moved to Frankfurt am Main when Martin Buber offered him a teaching position at the Jüdische Lehrhaus, an educational institute for Jewish adults. In addition to his duties at the Lehrhaus, Heschel lectured widely in the towns around Frankfurt, and tutored Buber in modern Hebrew. Meanwhile, keenly aware of the rising anti-Semitism in Germany, he actively sought to find an academic position elsewhere. An invitation to work at Hebrew Union College in Cincinnati eventually did arrive, but he faced delays in obtaining a visa. Before dawn on October 28, 1938, police agents entered his apartment and deported him – along with thousands of others – to Poland. He was thirty-one years old.

In Poland, Heschel continued to struggle to procure visas for himself, his mother, and three of his sisters. Concluding that he would be better positioned to secure the visas in England, he went to London in July 1939. A month later Germany invaded Poland and World War II broke out, preventing him from getting his relatives out of Poland. They were murdered in the Holocaust.

Heschel arrived in the United States in 1940. He lived in a dormitory while teaching at the Hebrew Union College in Cincinnati. When not writing academic studies or coping with teaching Judaica to American students who had little knowledge of Hebrew, he mastered the English language. Indeed, within a year of moving to the United States, he was already astonishing people with the eloquence of his written English.

In 1945, he joined the faculty at the Jewish Theological Seminary in New York, the hub of Conservative Judaism. The next year he married the classical pianist, Sylvia Straus. They had a daughter, Susannah, who is today an internationally celebrated scholar in Jewish studies.

Heschel wrote with great intensity during the late 1940s and early 1950s, publishing numerous influential

works including *The Earth is the Lord's*, *The Sabbath*,
and *Man's Quest for God*. The major treatise *Man Is Not
Alone* was published in 1951. While already well-known
in Jewish circles, he achieved national renown when
the famed Christian theologian, Reinhold Niebuhr,
reviewed it for the *New York Herald Tribune*, predict-
ing that Heschel would "become a commanding and
authoritative voice not only in the Jewish community
but in the religious life of America." During this period,
Heschel became increasingly prominent as a scholar and
theologian, and his work was admired and discussed by
many significant theologians, both Jewish and Christian.
He received a Guggenheim Fellowship in 1954 to write a
biography of the Baal Shem Tov, the legendary founder
of Hasidism, though he never finished the work. The
fellowship, however, did allow him to complete the
massive *God in Search of Man*. Unfortunately, the success
and fame that Heschel achieved was met with jealousy
and resentment by many of his colleagues at the Jewish
Theological Seminary.

In works from this fecund period of his career,
Heschel challenges the sensibilities of the modern West,
which emphasize detachment and disinterestedness,
viewing human reason as sufficient to understand all

that there is. In contrast, Heschel insists that for matters of ultimate concern, reason is inadequate. It is not reason but wonder and awe that open us to the vastness of the universe, which make us receptive to the deepest aspects of reality that are accessible to us.

In these works, among other things, Heschel seeks to upend the standard approach to the philosophy of religion. Philosophy of religion is too beholden to the "common sense" view of things, where meaning consists only in what we knowing selves bestow upon the world through our minds. Heschel seeks to displace this distinctly modern way of experiencing the world by reconstituting philosophy of religion on the basis of the experiences and sensibilities of the pious person. For the pious person, God is not an object to be known. Rather, God's overwhelming reality takes priority to the human mind's judgments. It is not for the human mind to render a verdict as to whether or not God exists, but rather, it is God who bestows meaning on everything, including the human self. Heschel is trying to evoke a sense that human beings are situated in much grander horizons than they realize, that there is a judge and center of meaning apart from and beyond our own minds. Philosophy of religion conducted in this manner, then, celebrates humility before the divine, since the awareness of God's overwhelming priority decenters us and puts us in our proper place.

In Heschel's view, the forfeiture of piety that has taken place in modernity, this loss of wonder and awe, has been disastrous for Western civilization. The atrocities of the twentieth century – the Holocaust prominent among them – are indicators of this debasement of culture and value. The segregation of religion into a private sphere, away from ethics and politics, is artificial and dangerous. Religion, when properly grasped, is inextricably bound to justice, and therefore it is of public, not merely personal, interest. If this rhetoric seems similar to that employed by religious conservatives in the so-called culture wars of recent history, it is important to recognize that Heschel did not view religion through a nostalgic lens, as a means to uphold the status quo. Rather, as he saw it, religion constitutes a radical challenge to the manner in which we conduct ourselves in daily life. For him, this challenge underlay a progressive politics based on his faith's recognition of human dignity.

During the 1950s, Heschel brought the fervor of the prophets to his role as a public intellectual. He delivered lectures to rabbinical organizations and synagogues and soon was invited to lecture at national forums, including the White House Conference on Children and Youth. In January 1963 he delivered a keynote address at the opening plenary session of the National Conference on Religion and Race in Chicago. In his address, he framed contemporary race relations in biblical terms, and denounced racism as satanic. Heschel's insights in *Die Prophetie*, which had recently been expanded and translated into English, took on a new resonance in the United States during the civil rights movement. The talk was passionate, reflecting his own experience with anti-Semitism in Europe and his observations of racism in Cincinnati and New York.

Heschel's denunciation of racism evoked the prophetic tradition he had written about. "Prophecy is the voice that God has lent to the silent agony, a voice to the plundered poor, to the profaned riches of the world." Anywhere injustice takes place, Heschel said, "few are guilty, but all are responsible." We are all responsible for evil because only a world indifferent to suffering will tolerate injustice and systematic inequality. Thus, "indifference to evil is more insidious than evil itself."

Yet so often injustice is simply accepted as the way things are. We remain unmoved, as if nothing calamitous were happening in our midst. Heschel understood the United States to be undergoing a terrible spiritual crisis. In his 1963 address for the Chicago conference, he provocatively asked, "The Negro's plight, the blighted areas in the large cities, are they not the fruit of our sins?" He suggested that we are accessories to this injustice by our failure "to demand, to insist, to challenge, to chastise," which is what true religion requires us to do.

Again, Heschel connected this failure to our loss of awe and wonder. "The root of sin is callousness, hardness of heart, lack of understanding what is at stake in being alive." When we lose sight of God's priorities and our place in the order of things, we become indifferent to our fellow human beings. Atrocities such as the Holocaust and the rampant poverty and racism in the United States happen because human beings close off the world to God and force God into hiding.

At the Chicago conference, Heschel first met Martin Luther King Jr., who also gave a plenary address. The two quickly became friends and frequently collaborated. After the police assault on nonviolent black protestors in Selma, Alabama, on March 7, 1965, Heschel began participating in rallies and protests. It was not long before he was included on an FBI list of citizens to monitor. Heschel took part in the famous march from Selma to Montgomery, alongside King and other civil rights leaders.

During this time, Heschel was actively engaged in a number of other issues, including protesting the Vietnam War, advocating on the behalf of Soviet Jewry, and consulting with the Vatican officials drafting *Nostra aetate*. Heschel worked closely with Augustin Cardinal Bea on the formulation of this declaration, the first of its kind, which emphasized the commonalities and shared commitments between Catholics and Jews. He was the most visible traditional Jew in the anti-Vietnam War movement, working alongside luminaries including Richard John Neuhaus, Daniel Berrigan, William Sloane Coffin Jr., and Robert McAfee Brown. Heschel played an important role in paving the way for King's address at the Riverside Church on the Vietnam War and American militarism. Heschel's engagement with these issues was not uncontroversial among American Jews. Many worried that if Jews were too visible in opposition to the Vietnam War, it would result in the United States withdrawing support from Israel. Others were critical of Heschel's collaboration with Christians.

Before his death in June 1971, Reinhold Niebuhr asked Heschel to deliver the eulogy at his funeral. According to Ursula Niebuhr, Heschel was her husband's closest friend in the last twelve years of his life.

When Heschel died in 1972, he left a behind a significant legacy. It is striking how many prominent voices in Jewish thought today were his students and present themselves as continuing his legacy. It is also striking that these students tend to gravitate to opposing ends of the political spectrum. Heschel's own thought is deeply inimical to the conceptual binaries between right and left, conservatism and liberalism, that characterize our thinking today. His work rejects the all-too-easy equation of "tradition" with conservative politics and insists upon the theological stakes of the everyday business of the public square. At this precarious moment in history, with increasing political polarization, declining commitments to democracy, staggering economic inequality, forced migrations, and serious human rights abuses, Heschel's writings are not merely relevant, they are urgent. In contrast to the emphasis on ideological purity and virtue signaling that drive so much political and cultural discourse, Heschel challenges us to attend to our own tendencies to deceive ourselves, and to recognize that self-righteousness often serves as a cover for indifference. To attain political and economic justice, a spiritual revolution is required.

Robert Erlewine is the Isaac Funk Professor of Religion at Illinois Wesleyan University and the author of *Monotheism and Tolerance* and *Judaism and the West*.

Reading Abraham Joshua Heschel Today

Susannah Heschel

WE LIVE IN AN AGE OF DESPAIR, and those who despair would seem justified, considering the compounding crises we face, whether they be economic, viral, political, or environmental. Yet despair, my father used to remind me, is forbidden; to despair is to deny that God is present, with us, caring for us, and that there is no challenge we are given without the resources to cope. My father, Abraham Joshua Heschel, is one of those resources. He speaks in the prophetic tradition of hope. The prophets know that unless we understand the very depths of corruption, misery, and despair, the hope we offer is superficial. Only the prophet who gives voice to the silent agony, who rages against injustice, whose passion exudes from every word, can offer true hope that "evil is never the climax of history," that redemption will come.

According to my father, the crises we face today are also a religious problem: "the systematic liquidation of man's sensitivity to the challenge of God." With that phrase, my father defines the purpose of his life's efforts.

Religion begins with a sense of embarrassment, he writes in his book *Who Is Man*, "the awareness of the incongruity of character and challenge, of perceptivity and reality, of knowledge and understanding, of mystery and comprehension." He used to say, "God begins where words end." In order to pray we need a refinement of the inner life, a sharpened conscience, a recognition that "prayer is action, an event."

"The beginning of wisdom is awe of God," the Bible often states, which my father translates: Embarrassment, loss of face, is the beginning of faith; it will make room within us. Religious people can never be self-assured or complacent; they can never say, "I am a good person," because they are constantly striving. He writes, "I am afraid of people who are never embarrassed at their own pettiness, prejudices, envy, and conceit, never embarrassed at the profanation of life." Embarrassment is meant to be productive; an end to embarrassment would bring a callousness that would threaten our humanity.

Yet my father did not stop with embarrassment, nor did he view religion as a form of self-abasement. On the contrary, religion is an awareness that God needs us. God is waiting for us, he writes in his book *God in Search of Man*. Like Abraham, who found God by contemplating nature, we, too, can sense God in the marvels of nature. We can also come to awareness of God through the Bible, and through study, to which my father was devoted in every spare moment. And then there are sacred deeds. What makes a deed sacred? In a striking passage in his book *The Sabbath*, he points out that we make the Sabbath holy: "The Sabbath is the presence of God in the world, open to the soul of man." Holy deeds are the mitzvot (commandments) of Torah, including prayer. The mitzvot, he writes, are prayers in the form of deeds. When my father returned from the 1965 civil rights march in Selma he said, "I felt my legs were praying." For him, marching for justice for black Americans was holy, an act of prayer.

Awareness of God is a challenge. It leads us to recognize that our life is not merely a gift but also a mandate to make our lives witnesses to God. Indeed, our lives are precisely what brings God into our world. An old Hasidic teaching he often quotes says that someone came to a rebbe to ask, "Where is God?" to which the rebbe answered, "Does not the psalmist say, 'The whole earth is filled with God's glory?' God is where you let God enter." In his book *The Earth Is the Lord's* my father writes, "In the days of Moses, Israel had a revelation of God; in the days of the Baal Shem (the founder of Hasidism), God had a revelation of Israel. Suddenly, there was revealed a holiness in Jewish life that had accumulated in the course of many generations." If to be a human being, created in God's image, means living a life that will serve to others as a reminder of God, then the purpose of Jewish life is to offer God a revelation of human holiness.

How do we let God enter? My father used to tease his audiences at a lecture, "When did God break the Ten Commandments?" The listeners were puzzled; he would then answer, "The Ten Commandments says, 'Thou shalt not make an image of God.' Yet God created us in his image." We are, he pointed out, the only image of God that we have. To live as an image of God is to live so that those who come to know us are reminded of God. My father often quotes an old Midrash (rabbinic commentary), "I am God and you are my witnesses; if you are not my witnesses, then I am not God."

My father places no limitations on this mandate to live as a witness to God; there is no singular path of a particular religion, nor is there a particular way to live as a Jew. In *Man Is Not Alone*, he draws on an old rabbinic teaching that divine revelation is an experience of God that is different for each person. The Torah comes to each of us, a revelation of God that we receive, each in a unique way, renewed every day. No single path leads to God because one's religion must be authentic to who we are. Since each person is unique, each expression will be as well. One cannot be Jewish the way one's grandparents were Jewish; that would be spiritual plagiarism: "A vibrant society does not dwell in the shadows of old ideas and viewpoints; in the realm of the spirit, only a pioneer can be a true heir. The wages of spiritual plagiarism are the loss of integrity; self-aggrandizement is self-betrayal. Authentic faith is more than an echo of a tradition. It is a creative situation, an event."

That our religiosity must be authentic to who we are as individuals is an old Hasidic teaching from Menachem Mendel, the rebbe of Kotzk, about whom my father wrote a two-volume book in Yiddish. The Kotzker rebbe, a complex and highly original thinker, insisted on truth, sincerity, and authenticity and loathed mendacity. My father wrote that book toward the end of his life, during the years he was active against the war in Vietnam. That war made him sick: he was outraged over the lies of American politicians and the callousness of a government killing thousands of innocent civilians. Yet why were Americans deceived by falsehoods of their government? The lies of politicians were abhorrent, but so was the gullibility of Americans. This was a religious problem, my father felt; people can want to be deceived. Do not deceive, the Kotzker rebbe insisted, and that also means do not deceive oneself by being gullible.

My father was unique among Jewish thinkers and scholars in his mastery of the full range of Jewish texts and ideas, from the Bible to rabbinics, kabbalah, philosophy, Hasidism, and modern scholarship. I know of no one else who has ever been able to cover that range and do so in four languages, in books and articles written for scholars and for a general audience, for Jews Christians, Muslims, and even atheists. Seen in historical perspective, my father would find it extraordinary that the writings of a Jewish theologian would find such resonance around the world: A Jew has brought them closer to God, deeper in their prayer, strengthened in their faith.

In fact, he often said that he felt he was better understood by Christians than by Jews. Christians had a long tradition of theological discussion, whereas many Jews had turned away from theology, preferring political analyses of Jewish identity, or focusing on "customs and ceremonies," words my father wanted erased from our vocabulary. Where was genuine piety to be found? My father grew up, he said, surrounded by people of "religious nobility" – an extraordinary phrase. That entire world that nurtured him was destroyed by the Nazis. In America, Judaism was something different, and he was sharply critical of the forms it took. The synagogue, he said, is where prayer goes to die. Congregants sit back in their pews and let the rabbi and cantor conduct "vicarious praying." Sermons are superficial, failing to recognize the genuine anguish of those who come to pray. Too many people leave the synagogue just as they entered, feeling good about themselves, whereas prayer, he wrote, should be subversive. We don't pray in order to achieve something else, he said, "we pray in order to pray," to open a door to God, who is "a refugee in his own world." If there is any hope for the future of Judaism in America, my father used to say, it lies with the black church. That is where he felt the spirit he had known in Eastern Europe.

Hasidism inspired my father's religiosity and also his social activism. Descended from some of the most important Hasidic rebbes for many generations, my father learned from them the true depths of empathy and the great efforts of rebbes to lift people out of despair and restore to them the joy of being a Jew. Empathy was central to the prophets, too, he argued: "The prophet's ear perceives the silent sigh" of human suffering. "The prophet's word is a scream in the night. While the world is at ease and asleep, the prophet feels the blast from heaven." In speaking on behalf of the silent, the prophet is also expressing God's empathy, or what my father calls "divine pathos." It is God's profound concern for humanity, indeed God's suffering in response to ours, that the prophet comes to convey: "The prophet hears God's voice and feels his heart."

How do we live in the prophetic spirit? After all, my father said so often, "some are guilty, but all are responsible." Faith is a challenge that requires a prophetic response from us, involvement in the lives of other human beings: "Man insists not only on being satisfied but also on being able to satisfy, on being needed, not only on having needs. Personal needs come and go, but one anxiety remains: Am I needed?" The prophet answers: Yes, profoundly.

My father always saw experiences in historical perspective, reminding me, for example, of the extraordinary breakthrough represented by *Nostra aetate*; when had the church ever spoken in such positive words about Judaism? At the same time, he was not insistent on retaining tradition at all costs. He suggested that I become a rabbi, telling me that he believed things would change and women might one day become rabbis.

When I think of the Sabbath observances in my parents' home, I feel the sacredness of that day. My father knew how to create a moment pregnant with significance, and he once wrote, "It takes three things to create a sense of significant being: God, a soul, and a moment. And the three are always present." Always remember that God needs us, that we are an object of divine concern. For my father, that is the heart of religious faith.

Modernity promised us that we could overcome ignorance and achieve great things, if only we would emerge from the tutelage of others and use our reason. By now we have discovered that man cannot live by reason alone; many thinkers, including my father, have pointed to the rationalization that underlay Auschwitz and Hiroshima. What has happened to our sense of wonder, of mystery, of the ineffable, all of which have been suppressed as unnecessary to a modern age, yet all of which are essential to our humanity? The obligation falls upon us to foster in ourselves the sensibilities that modernity has suppressed or even denigrated. For example, he writes that we look at nature and see its power, beauty, and grandeur. How do we respond? We exploit and we enjoy, but do we stand in awe? Without awe, our lives are impoverished, our society decays.

For my father, it is not that we need religion; it is that our very humanity can only come into fullness if we give our souls a chance to express themselves. Only in prayer can we speak our deepest yearnings. We are born human, but prayer challenges us to remember that we shape ourselves as human beings.

While we live in the present, we also live in biblical time: that is a guiding principle of Jewish and Christian liturgy that imbues my father's writings. At the Passover Seder, the Haggadah reminds us that we must see ourselves as though we, too, have gone forth from Egypt. In interreligious dialogue, he identified himself biblically: "I speak as a member of a congregation whose founder was Abraham, and the name of my rabbi is Moses." Speaking at a conference on religion and race in 1963, he opened by stating, "At the first summit on religion and race, the main participants were Pharaoh and Moses." He went on to declare, "Racism is satanism, unmitigated evil," becoming one of the strongest white voices for racial justice. He was horrified to flee Nazi Germany's anti-Semitism and find rampant racism in a country dedicated to democratic ideals. He would inveigh again and again, in talks to a variety of audiences, that racism is not just wrong, it diminishes our humanity, denies God as the creator, and shatters every principle of the Bible. Already then, he understood the systemic nature of racism, how it is institutionalized in an economy that forces some people into horrendous poverty, and in laws that function as barriers to the institutions that are supposed to be guaranteed rights of education, housing, and medical care. He enjoined Martin Luther King Jr. to speak out against the war in Vietnam, which both of them viewed as a force of racism in American society.

My father did not write for one group or one faith; he wrote for all of us. Most important are the questions my father poses as central to interreligious encounter. We share so many problems that affect all of us, regardless of our religious affiliation; racism is a religious problem, as is war, poverty, nuclear weaponry, or injustice. These are religious problems for all of us.

Within our faiths, we also have problems: "No religion, magnificent as it may be, can survive without repair from time to time." Together we have to face the callousness that has overtaken us; the opposite of good, he writes, is not evil but indifference.

At the conclusion of his extraordinary lecture, "No Religion Is an Island," my father asks, "What is the purpose of interreligious dialogue?" He answers his own question:

It is neither to flatter nor to refute one another, but to help one another, to share insight and learning, to cooperate in academic ventures on the highest scholarly level and, what is even more important, to search in the wilderness for wellsprings of devotion, for treasures of stillness, for the power of love and care for man. What is urgently needed are ways of helping one another in the terrible predicament of here and now by the courage to believe that the word of the Lord endures forever as well as here and now; to cooperate in trying to bring about a resurrection of sensitivity, a revival of conscience; to keep alive the divine sparks in our souls; to nurture openness to the spirit of the Psalms, reverence for the words of the prophets, and faithfulness to the Living God.

Susannah Heschel, the only child of Abraham Joshua Heschel, is the Eli Black Professor of Jewish Studies at Dartmouth College and the editor of *Moral Grandeur and Spiritual Audacity: Essays of Abraham Joshua Heschel.*

I

Every Moment Touches Eternity

NOT THE INDIVIDUAL MAN, nor a single generation by its own power, can erect the bridge that leads to God. Faith is the achievement of ages, an effort accumulated over centuries. Many of its ideas are as the light of a star that left its source centuries ago. Many songs, unfathomable today, are the resonance of voices of bygone times. There is a collective memory of God in the human spirit, and it is this memory of which we partake in our faith. . . .

The riches of a soul are stored up in its memory. This is the test of character – not whether a man follows the daily fashion, but whether the past is alive in his present. When we want to understand ourselves, to find out what is most precious in our lives, we search our memory. Memory is the soul's witness to the capricious mind.

Only those who are spiritually imitators, only people who are afraid to be grateful and too weak to be loyal, have nothing but the present moment. To a noble person it is a holy joy to remember, an overwhelming thrill to be grateful, while to a person whose character is neither rich nor strong, gratitude is a most painful sensation. The secret of wisdom is never to get lost in a momentary mood or passion, never to forget friendship because of a momentary grievance, never to lose sight of the lasting values because of a transitory episode. The things which sweep through our daily life should be valued according to whether or not they enrich the inner cistern. That only is valuable in our experience which is worth remembering. Remembrance is the touchstone of all actions.

Memory is a source of faith. To have faith is to remember. Jewish faith is a recollection of that which happened to Israel in the past. The events in which the spirit of God became a reality stand before our eyes painted in colors that never fade. Much of what the Bible demands can be comprised in one word: *Remember.* "Take heed to thyself, and keep thy soul diligently lest thou forget the things which thine eyes saw, and lest they depart from thy heart all the days of thy life; make them known unto thy children and thy children's children" (Deut. 4:9).

Jews have not preserved the ancient monuments, they have retained the ancient moments. The light kindled in their history was never extinguished. With sustaining vitality the past survives in their thoughts, hearts, rituals. Recollection is a holy act: we sanctify the present by remembering the past.

TO HAVE FAITH does not mean, however, to dwell in the shadow of old ideas conceived by prophets and sages, to live off an inherited estate of doctrines and dogmas. In the realm of spirit only he who is a pioneer is able to be an heir. The wages of spiritual plagiarism is the loss of integrity; self-aggrandizement is self-betrayal.

Authentic faith is more than an echo of a tradition. It is a creative situation, an event. For God is not always silent, and man is not always blind. In every man's life there are moments when there is a lifting of the veil at the horizon of the known, opening a sight of the eternal. Each of us has at least once in his life experienced the momentous reality of God. Each of us has once caught a glimpse of the beauty, peace, and power that flow through the souls of those who are devoted to Him.

But such experiences or inspirations are rare events. To some people they are like shooting stars, passing and unremembered. In others they kindle a light that is never quenched. The remembrance of that experience and the loyalty to the response of that moment are the forces that sustain our faith. In this sense, *faith is faithfulness*, loyalty to an event, loyalty to our response.

THE WAY TO THE LASTING does not lie on the other side of life; it does not begin where time breaks off. The lasting begins not beyond but *within time*, within the moment, within the concrete. Time can be seen from two aspects: from the aspect of *temporality* and from the aspect of *eternity*.

Time is the border of eternity. Time is eternity formed into tassels. The moments of our lives are like luxuriant tassels. They are attached to the garment and are made of the same cloth. It is through spiritual living that we realize that the infinite can be confined in a measured line.

Life without integrity is like loosely hanging threads, easily straying from the main cloth, while in acts of piety we learn to understand that every instant is like a thread raveling out of eternity to form a delicate tassel. We must not cast off the threads but weave them into the design of an eternal fabric.

The days of our lives are representatives of eternity rather than fugitives, and we must live as if the fate of all of time would totally depend on a single moment.

Seen as temporality, the essence of time is detachment, isolation. A temporal moment is always alone, always exclusive. Two instants can never be together, never contemporary. Seen as eternity, the essence of time is attachment, communion. It is within time rather than within space that we are able to commune, to worship, to love. It is within time that one day may be worth a thousand years.

Creative insights grow a lifetime to last a moment, and yet they last forever. For to last means to commune with God, "to cleave unto Him" (Deut. 11:22). A moment has no contemporary within temporality. But within eternity every moment can become a contemporary of God.

LITTLE IS RECORDED or remembered either about the life and character of Euclid or about the way in which his *Elements* came into being. The laws of his geometry are timeless, and the moment in which they first dawned upon the human mind seems to have no bearing upon their meaning and validity. Time and thought, act and content, author and teaching, are not related to each other.

In contrast, the words of the Bible are not suspended; they do not dangle in an air of timelessness. Here time and thought, act and content, author and teaching, are profoundly related to each other.

The Bible is not only a system of norms but also a record of happenings in history. Indeed, some of the biblical maxims and principles may be found or could have been conceived elsewhere. Without parallel in the world are the events it tells us about and the fact of taking these events as the points where God and man meet. Events are among the basic categories by which the biblical man lives; they are to his existence what axioms are to measuring and weighing.

Judaism is *a religion of history, a religion of time*. The God of Israel was not found primarily in the facts of nature. He spoke through events in history. While the deities of other peoples were associated with places or things, the God of the prophets was the God of events: the Redeemer from slavery, the Revealer of the Torah, manifesting Himself in events of history rather than in things or places.

The events from which the religion of Israel is derived, the particular moments in time in which God and man met are as fundamental to Judaism as the eternity of divine justice and compassion and the general truth that God and man stand at all times in relation to each other. To maintain that the exodus from Egypt is a symbol only, that the essential point is the general idea of liberty which the story signifies is to disregard the heart of Jewish faith.

Judaism demands the acceptance of some basic thoughts or norms as well as attachment to some decisive events. Its ideas and its events are inseparable from each other. The spirit manifests itself through God's presence in history, and the acts of manifestation are verified through basic thoughts or norms.

TO MOST OF US the idea of revelation is unacceptable, not because it cannot be proved or explained, but because it is *unprecedented*. We do not even reject it, it simply does not enter our minds; we possess no form or category in which that idea could take hold. Trained in seeking to explain all that happens as a manifestation of a general law, every phenomenon as an example of a type, we find it hard to believe in the extraordinary, in the absolutely

7

singular; we find it hard to believe that an event which does not happen *all the time* or from time to time should have happened only *once, at one time*. It is taken for granted in science that in the realm of space a process which happened once can happen all the time, but we have not the power to understand that in the realm of time certain events do not happen again and again. Now, revelation is an event that does not happen all the time but at a particular time, at a unique moment of time.

No other deficiency makes the soul more barren than the lack of a sense for the unique. The creative man is he who succeeds in capturing the exceptional and instantaneous before it becomes stagnant in his mind. In the language of creative thinking, whatever is alive is unique. And true insight is a moment of perceiving a situation before it freezes into similarity with something else.

Only genius knows how to communicate to others the sense of the instantaneous and unique, and even so the poetry of all ages has captured a mere fraction of the endless music of the incomparable. There is more discernment in sensing the ineffable uniqueness of an event than in trying to explain it away by our stereotyped doubts.

Just as there are ideas which are true, though only a few people are able to corroborate or verify them, there are experiences which are real, though only a few people are able to attain them. Many things occur between God and man which escape the attention even of those to whom they happen.

UNLESS WE LEARN how to appreciate and distinguish moments of time as we do things of space, unless we become sensitive to the uniqueness of individual events, the meaning of revelation will remain obscure. Indeed, uniqueness is a category that belongs more to the realm of time than to the realm of space. Two stones, two things in space may be alike; two hours in a person's life or two ages in human history are never alike. What happened once will never happen again in the same sense. The age of Pericles or the period of the Renaissance were never duplicated. It is ignorance of time, unawareness of the depth of events that leads to the claim that history repeats itself. It is because of his profound sense of time that the biblical man was able to comprehend that at Sinai* he witnessed an event without parallel in human history. . . .

* The revelation of God at Mount Sinai is a central event in the Jewish understanding of the Bible because it is the moment when God forms a covenant with the Jewish people.

The lack of realism, the insistence upon generalizations at the price of a total disregard of the particular and the concrete is something which would be alien to prophetic thinking. Prophetic words are never detached from the concrete, historic situation. Theirs is not a timeless, abstract message; it always refers to an actual situation. The general is given in the particular, and the verification of the abstract is in the concrete.

Judaism does not seek to subordinate philosophy to events, timeless verities to a particular history. It tries to point to a level of reality where the events are the manifestations of divine norms, where history is understood as the fulfillment of truth.

The meaning of history is our profound concern. It is difficult to remain immune to the anxiety of the question, whence we come, where we are, and whither we are going.

IT IS IMPOSSIBLE for man to shirk the problem of time. The more we think the more we realize: we cannot conquer time through space. We can only master time in time.

The higher goal of spiritual living is not to amass a wealth of information, but to face sacred moments. In a religious experience, for example, it is not a thing that imposes itself on man but a spiritual presence. What is retained in the soul is the moment of insight rather than the place where the act came to pass. A moment of insight is a fortune, transporting us beyond the confines of measured time. Spiritual life begins to decay when we fail to sense the grandeur of what is eternal in time. . . .

Time and space are interrelated. To overlook either of them is to be partially blind. What we plead against is man's unconditional surrender to space, his enslavement to things. We must not forget that it is not a thing that lends significance to a moment; it is the moment that lends significance to things.

2

The Only Life Worth Living

AWARENESS OF A MYSTERY is shared by all people.
Yet, as we have seen, they usually mistake what they
sense as being apart from their own existence, as if there
were only wonder in what they see, not in the very act of
seeing, as if the mystery were merely an object of observa-
tion. Unsparing, unqualified thinking opens our minds
to the fact that the mystery is not apart from ourselves,
not a far-off thing like a rainbow in the sky; the mystery
is out of doors, in all things to be seen, not only where
there is more than what the senses can grasp. Those to
whom awareness of the ineffable is a constant state of
mind know that the mystery is not an exception but an

air that lies about all being, a spiritual setting of reality; not something apart but a *dimension* of all existence.

They learn to sense that all existence is embraced by *spiritual presence*; that life is not a property of the self; that the world is an open house in which the presence of the owner is so well concealed that we usually mistake His discretion for nonexistence.

There is a holiness that hovers over all things, that makes them look to us in some moments like objects of transcendent meditation, as if *to be* meant *to be thought of* by God, as if all external life were embraced by an inner life, by a process within a mind, pensive, intentional. . . .

To the religious man it is as if things stood with *their back to him, their faces turned to God*, as if the ineffable quality of things consisted in their being an object of divine thought. Just as in touching a tree we know that the tree is not the end of the world, that the tree stands in space, so we know that the ineffable – what is holy in justice, compassion, and truthfulness – is not the end of spirit; that the ultimate values survive our misjudgments, deflations, and repudiations; that meaning is meaningful not because of our minds; that beauty is beautiful not by the grace of man.

The soul is introduced to a reality which is not only *other* than itself, as it is the case in the ordinary acts of perception; it is introduced to a reality which is *higher* than the universe. Our soul compares with its glory as a breath with all the world's air. We are introduced to a reality, the mere awareness of which is more precious to us than our own existence. The thought of it is too powerful to be ignored and too holy to be absorbed by us. It is a thought in which we share. It is as if the human mind were not alone in thinking it, but the whole universe were full of it. We don't wonder *at* things anymore; we wonder *with* all things. We do not think about things; we think for all things.

PIETY POINTS TO SOMETHING beyond itself. As it works in the inner life, it keeps ever referring us to something that transcends man, something that goes beyond the present instant, something that surmounts what is visible and available. Steadily preventing man from immersing himself in sensation or ambition, it stands staunchly as the champion of something more important than interest and desires, than passion or career. While not denying the charm and beauty of the world, the pious man realizes that life takes place under wide horizons,

horizons that range beyond the span of an individual life or even the life of a nation, of a generation, or even of an era. His sight perceives something indicative of the divine. In the small things he senses the significant; in the common and the simple he senses the ultimate; in the rush of the passing he feels the stillness of the eternal. While piety stands in relation to what man knows and feels about the horizons of life, it exceeds by far the sum total reached by adding up his diverse intellectual and emotional experiences. Its essence, in fact, stands for something more than a theory, a sentiment, or a conviction. To those who adhere to it, piety is compliance with destiny, the only life worth living, the only course of life that does not eventually throw man into bestial chaos.

Piety is thus a mode of living. It is the orientation of human inwardness toward the holy. It is a predominant interest in the ultimate value of all acts, feelings, and thoughts. With his heart open to and attracted by some spiritual gravitation, the pious man moves, as it were, toward the center of a universal stillness, and his conscience is so placed as to listen to the voice of God.

Every man's life is dominated by certain interests and is essentially determined by the aspiration toward those things which matter to him most. The pious man's main interest is concern for the concern of God, which thus becomes the driving force controlling the course of his actions and decisions, molding his aspirations and behavior. It is fallacious to see in isolated acts of perception or consideration the decisive elements in human behavior. Actually, it is the direction of mind and heart, the general interest of a person, that leads him to see or discover certain situations and to overlook others. Interest is . . . a selective apprehension based on prior ideas, preceding insights, recognitions, or predilections. The interest of a pious man is determined by his faith, so that piety is faith translated into life, spirit embodied in a personality.

PIETY IS AN ATTITUDE toward all of reality. The pious man is alert to the dignity of every human being, and to those bearings upon the spiritual value which even inanimate things inalienably possess. Being able to sense the relations of things to transcendent values, he will be incapable of disparaging any of them by enslaving them to his own service. The secret of every being is the divine care and concern that are invested in it. In every event there is something sacred at stake, and it is for this reason that the approach of the pious man to reality is in reverence. This explains his solemnity and his conscientiousness in dealing with things both great and small.

STANDING FACE TO FACE with the world, we often sense a spirit which surpasses our ability to comprehend. The world is too much for us. It is crammed with marvel. The glory is not an exception but an aura that lies about all being, a spiritual setting of reality.

3

In the Presence of Mystery

ALWAYS WE ARE CHASING WORDS, and always words recede. But the greatest experiences are those for which we have no expression. To live only on that which we can say is to wallow in the dust, instead of digging up the soil. How shall we ignore the mystery, in which we are involved, to which we are attached by our very existence? How shall we remain deaf to the throb of the cosmic that is subtly echoed in our own souls? The most intimate is the most mysterious. Wonder alone is the compass that may direct us to the pole of meaning. As I enter the next second of my life, while writing these lines, I am aware that to be swept by the enigma and to pause – rather than to flee and to forget – is to live within the core.

To become aware of the ineffable is to part company with words. The essence, the tangent to the curve of human experience, lies beyond the limits of language. The world of things we perceive is but a veil. Its flutter is music, its ornament science, but what it conceals is inscrutable. Its silence remains unbroken; no words can carry it away.

Sometimes we wish the world could cry and tell us about that which made it pregnant with fear-filling grandeur. Sometimes we wish our own heart would speak of that which made it heavy with wonder.

REVERENCE IS AN ATTITUDE as indigenous to human consciousness as fear when facing danger or pain when hurt. The scope of revered objects may vary; reverence itself is characteristic of man in all civilizations. Let us analyze a rather common and perhaps universal example of such an attitude, the inner structure of which will prove to be the same in all examples – whatever the object revered may be. Obviously, we can never sneer at the stars, mock the dawn, or scoff at the totality of being. Sublime grandeur evokes unhesitating, unflinching awe.

Away from the immense, cloistered in our own concepts, we may scorn and revile everything. But standing between earth and sky, we are silenced by the sight. . . .

Reverence is one of man's answers to the presence of the mystery. This is why, in contradistinction to other emotions, it does not rush to be spoken. When we stand in awe, our lips do not demand speech; we know that if we spoke, we would deprave ourselves. In such moments talk is an abomination. All we want is to pause, to be still, that the moment may last. It is like listening to great music; how it reaps the yield from the fertile soil of stillness; we are swept by it without being able to appraise it. The meaning of the things we revere is overwhelming and beyond the grasp of our understanding. We possess no categories for it and would distort it if we tried to appraise it by our standard of values; it essentially surpasses our criteria.

WE ARE RARELY AWARE of the tangent of the beyond at the whirling wheel of experience. In our passion for knowledge, our minds prey upon the wealth of an unresisting world and, seizing our limited spoils, we quickly leave the ground to lose ourselves in the whirlwind of our own knowledge.

The horizon of knowledge is lost in the mist produced by fads and phrases. We refuse to take notice of what is beyond our sight, content with converting realities into opinions, mysteries into dogmas, and ideas into a multitude of words. What is extraordinary appears to us habit, the dawn a daily routine of nature. But time and again we awake. In the midst of walking in the never-ending procession of days and nights, we are suddenly filled with a solemn terror, with a feeling of our wisdom being inferior to dust. We cannot endure the heartbreaking splendor of sunsets. Of what avail, then, are opinions, words, dogmas? In the confinement of our study rooms, our knowledge seems to us a pillar of light. But when we stand at the door which opens out to the infinite, we realize that all concepts are but glittering motes that populate a sunbeam.

To some of us, explanations and opinions are tokens of the wonder's departure, like a curfew ringing the end of insight and search. However, those to whom reality is dearer than information, to whom life is stronger than concepts and the world more than words, are never deluded into believing that what they know and perceive is the core of reality. We are able to exploit, to label things with well-trimmed words; but when ceasing to subject them to our purposes and to impose on them the forms of our intellect, we are stunned and incapable of saying what things are in themselves; it is an experience of being unable to experience something we face: too great to be perceived. Music, poetry, religion – they all initiate in the soul's encounter with an aspect of reality for which reason has no concepts and language has no names.

THE BEGINNING OF FAITH is not a feeling for the mystery of living or a sense of awe, wonder, or fear. The root of religion is the question of what to do with the feeling for the mystery of living, what to do with awe, wonder, or fear. Religion, the end of isolation, begins with a consciousness that something is asked of us. It is in that tense, eternal asking in which the soul is caught and in which man's answer is elicited.

Wonder is not a state of esthetic enjoyment. Endless wonder is endless tension, a situation in which we are shocked at the inadequacy of our awe, at the weakness of our shock, as well as the state of being asked the ultimate question.

Endless wonder unlocks an innate sense of indebtedness. Within our awe there is no place for self-assertion.

Within our awe we only know that all we own we owe. The world consists, not of things, but of tasks. Wonder is the state of our being asked. The ineffable is a question addressed to us.

All that is left to us is a choice – to answer or to refuse to answer. Yet the more deeply we listen, the more we become stripped of the arrogance and callousness which alone would enable us to refuse. We carry a load of marvel, wishing to exchange it for the simplicity of knowing what to live for, a load which we can never lay down nor continue to carry not knowing where.

At the moment in which a fire bursts forth, threatening to destroy one's home, a person does not pause to investigate whether the danger he faces is real or a figment of his imagination. Such a moment is not the time to inquire into the chemical principle of combustion, or into the question of who is to blame for the outbreak of the fire. The ultimate question, when bursting forth in our souls, is too startling, too heavily laden with unutterable wonder to be an academic question, to be equally suspended between yes and no. Such a moment is not the time to throw doubts upon the reason for the rise of the question.

THERE IS NO KNOWLEDGE that would be an answer to endless wonder, that could stem the tide of its silent challenge. When we are overtaken by endless wonder, all inference is an awkward retrogression; in such moments a syllogism is not self-evident, but an insight is. In such moments our logical affirmation, our saying yes, appears like a bubble of thought at the strand of an eternal sea. We, then, realize that our concern is not: What may we know? How could we open Him to our minds? Our concern is: To whom do we belong? How could we open our lives to Him?

Where self-assertion is no more; when realizing that wonder is not our own achievement; that it is not by our own power alone that we are shuddered with radical amazement, it is not within our power anymore to assume the role of an examiner of a subject in search of an object, such as we are in search of a cause when perceiving thunder. Ultimate wonder is not the same as curiosity. Curiosity is the state of a mind in search of knowledge, while ultimate wonder is the state of knowledge in search of a mind; it is the thought of God in search of a soul.

What is decisive is not the existential moment of despair, the acceptance of our own bankruptcy, but, on

24

the contrary, the realization of our great spiritual power, the power to heal what is broken in the world, the realization of our capacity to answer God's question.

THE FUNDAMENTALISTS CLAIM that all ultimate questions have been answered; the logical positivists maintain that all ultimate questions are meaningless. Those of us who share neither the conceit of the former nor the unconcern of the latter, and reject both specious answers and false evasions, know that an ultimate issue is at stake in our existence, the relevance of which surpasses all final formulations. It is this embarrassment that is the starting point for our thinking.

THE SENSE OF THE INEFFABLE, the awareness of the grandeur and mystery of living, is shared by all people, and it is in the depth of such awareness that acts and thoughts of religion are full of meaning. The ideas of religion are *an answer*, when the mystery is *a problem*. When brought to the level of utilitarian thinking, when their meaning is taken literally as solutions to scientific problems, they are bound to be meaningless. Thus the basic *ideas* in Judaism have more than one dimension; what they refer to is a mystery, and they become distorted when taken as matter-of-fact descriptions. The idea of man as a being created in the likeness of God, the idea of creation, of divine knowledge, the election of Israel, the problem of evil, messianism, the belief in the resurrection, or faith in revelation become caricatures when transposed into the categories of pedestrian thinking.

When Moses was about to depart from this world, he said, "Master of the Universe, I ask of Thee one favor before I die, that all the gates of both heaven and the abyss be opened, and people shall see that there is none beside Thee" (Deuteronomy Rabba 11:8). Moses' request was not granted, and the gates remained closed.

AWE IS A WAY OF BEING in rapport with the mystery of all reality. The awe that we sense or ought to sense when standing in the presence of a human being is a moment of intuition for the likeness of God which is concealed in his essence. Not only man; even inanimate things stand in a relation to the Creator. . . .

Awe is an intuition for the creaturely dignity of all things and their preciousness to God; a realization that things not only are what they are but also stand, however remotely, for something absolute. Awe is a sense for the transcendence, for the reference everywhere to Him who is beyond all things. It is an insight better conveyed in attitudes than in words. The more eager we are to express it, the less remains of it. . . .

In analyzing or evaluating an object, we think and judge from a particular point of view. The psychologist, economist, and chemist pay attention to different aspects of the same object. Such is the limitation of the mind that it can never see three sides of a building at the same time. The danger begins when, completely caught in one perspective, we attempt to consider a part as the whole. In the twilight of such perspectivism, even the sight of the part is distorted. What we cannot comprehend by analysis, we become aware of in awe. When we "stand still and consider," we face and witness what is immune to analysis.

Knowledge is fostered by curiosity; wisdom is fostered by awe. True wisdom is participation in the wisdom of God. Some people may regard as wisdom "an uncommon degree of common sense." To us, wisdom is the ability to look at all things from the point of view of God, sympathy with the divine pathos, the identification of the will with the will of God. "Thus says the Lord: Let not the wise man glory in his wisdom, let not the mighty man glory in his might, let not the rich man glory in his riches;

but let him who glories glory in this, that he understands and knows Me, that I am the Lord who practices kindness, justice, and righteousness on the earth; for in these things I delight, says the Lord" (Jer. 9:22–23).

THERE IS NO FAITH at first sight. A faith that comes into being like a butterfly is ephemeral. He who is swift to believe is swift to forget. Faith does not come into being out of nothing, inadvertently, unprepared, as an unearned surprise. Faith is preceded by awe, by acts of amazement at things that we apprehend but cannot comprehend. In the story of the Red Sea we read: "Israel *saw* the great works which the Lord did . . . and the people *feared* the Lord . . . and they *believed in the Lord*" (Exod. 14:31). We must learn how to see "the miracles which are daily with us"; we must learn how to live in awe, in order to attain the insights of faith.

"The thoughtless believes every word, but the prudent looks where he is going" (Prov. 14:15). The will to believe may be the will to power in disguise, yet the will to power and the will to believe are mutually exclusive. For in our striving for power we arrogate to ourselves what belongs to God and suppress the claim of His presence. We must learn how to let His will prevail. We must understand that our faith is not only our concern but also His; that more important than our will to believe is His will that we believe.

It is not easy to attain faith. A decision of the will, the desire to believe, will not secure it. All the days of our lives we must continue to deepen our sense of mystery in order to be worthy of attaining faith. Callousness to the mystery is our greatest obstacle. In the artificial light of pride and self-contentment we shall never see the splendor. Only *in His light shall we see the light.*

Man's quest for God is not a quest for mere information. In terms of information little was attained by those countless men who strained their minds to find an answer. Only in terms of responsiveness, as an answer to Him who asked, much was achieved and much can be achieved by every one of us. In the realm of science, a question may be asked and an answer given by one man for all men. In the realm of religion, the question must be faced and the answer given by every individual soul.

4

The Prophets Show Us God Cares

TO A PERSON ENDOWED with prophetic sight, everyone else appears blind; to a person whose ear perceives God's voice, everyone else appears deaf. No one is just; no knowing is strong enough, no trust complete enough. The prophet hates the approximate, he shuns the middle of the road. Man must live on the summit to avoid the abyss. There is nothing to hold to except God. Carried away by the challenge, the demand to straighten out man's ways, the prophet is strange, one-sided, an unbearable extremist.

Others may suffer from the terror of cosmic aloneness; the prophet is overwhelmed by the grandeur of divine presence. He is incapable of isolating the world. There is an interaction between man and God which to disregard is an act of insolence. Isolation is a fairy tale.

Where an idea is the father of faith, faith must conform to the ideas of the given system. In the Bible the realness of God came first, and the task was how to live in a way compatible with His presence. Man's coexistence with God determines the course of history.

The prophet disdains those for whom God's presence is comfort and security; to him it is a challenge, an incessant demand. God is compassion, not compromise; justice, though not inclemency. The prophet's predictions can always be proved wrong by a change in man's conduct, but never the certainty that God is full of compassion.

The prophet's word is a scream in the night. While the world is at ease and asleep, the prophet feels the blast from heaven.

THE PROPHET IS A WATCHMAN (Hos. 9:8), a servant (Amos 3:7; Jer. 25:4; 26:5), a messenger of God (Hag. 1:13), "an assayer and tester" of the people's ways (Jer. 6:27, RSV); "whenever you hear a word from My mouth, you shall give them warning from Me" (Ezek. 3:17). The prophet's eye is directed to the contemporary scene; the society and its conduct are the main theme of his speeches. Yet his ear is inclined to God. He is a person struck by the glory and presence of God, overpowered by the hand of God. Yet his true greatness is his ability to hold God and man in a single thought.

The spiritual status of a diviner, not to be confused with a prophet, is higher than that of his fellow man; the diviner is regarded as more exalted than other members of his society. However, the measure of such superiority is that of individuality. In contrast, the prophet feels himself placed not only above the other members of his own society; he is placed in a relationship transcending his own total community, and even the realm of other nations and kingdoms. The measure of his superiority is that of universality. This is why the essence of his eminence is not adequately described by the term *charisma*. . . .

The prophet claims to be far more than a messenger. He is a person who stands in the presence of God (Jer. 15:19), who stands "in the council of the Lord" (Jer. 23:18), who is a participant, as it were, in the council of God, not a bearer of dispatches whose function is limited to being sent on errands. . . .

The words the prophet utters are not offered as souvenirs. His speech to the people is not a reminiscence, a report, hearsay. The prophet not only conveys; he reveals. He almost does unto others what God does unto him. In speaking, the prophet reveals God. This is the marvel of a prophet's work: in his words, *the invisible God becomes audible.* He does not prove or argue. The thought he has to convey is more than language can contain. Divine power bursts in the words. The authority of the prophet is in the Presence his words reveal.

There are no proofs for the existence of the God of Abraham. There are only witnesses. The greatness of the prophet lies not only in the ideas he expressed, but also in the moments he experienced. The prophet is a witness, and his words a testimony – to *His* power and judgment, to *His* justice and mercy.

WHAT IS THE PRIMARY CONTENT of prophetic experience, the thought immediately felt, the motive directly present to the prophet's mind? What are the facts of consciousness that stirred him so deeply? Is it a sense of anxiety about the fate and future of the people or of the state? An impulse of patriotism? Is it personal irritation at the violation of moral laws and standards, a spontaneous reaction of the conscience against what is wrong or evil? Moral indignation?

In a stricken hour comes the word of the prophet. There is tension between God and man. What does the word say? What does the prophet feel? The prophet is not only a censurer and accuser, but also a defender and consoler. Indeed, the attitude he takes to the tension that obtains between God and the people is characterized by a dichotomy. In the presence of God he takes the part of the people. In the presence of the people he takes the part of God.

It would be wrong to maintain that the prophet is a person who plays the role of "the third party," offering his good offices to bring about reconciliation. His view is oblique. God is the focal point of his thought, and the world is seen as reflected in God. Indeed, the main task of prophetic thinking is to bring the world into divine focus. This, then, explains his way of thinking. He does not take a direct approach to things. It is not a straight line, spanning subject and object, but rather a triangle – through God to the object. An expression of a purely personal feeling betrays itself seldom, in isolated instances. The prophet is endowed with the insight that enables him to say, not I love or I condemn, but God loves or God condemns.

The prophet does not judge the people by timeless norms, but from the point of view of God. Prophecy proclaims what happened to God as well as what will happen to the people. In judging human affairs, it unfolds a divine situation. Sin is not only the violation of a law, it is as if sin were as much a loss to God as to man. God's role is not spectatorship but involvement. He and man meet mysteriously in the human deed. The prophet cannot say Man without thinking God.

Therefore, the prophetic speeches are not factual pronouncements. What we hear is not objective criticism or the cold proclamation of doom. The style of legal, objective utterance is alien to the prophet. He dwells upon God's inner motives, not only upon His historical decisions. He discloses *a divine pathos*, not just a divine judgment. The pages of the prophetic writings are filled with echoes of divine love and disappointment, mercy and indignation. The God of Israel is never impersonal.

This divine pathos is the key to inspired prophecy. God is involved in the life of man. A personal relation-ship binds Him to Israel; there is an interweaving of the divine in the affairs of the nation. The divine commandments are not mere recommendations for man, but express divine concern, which, realized or repudiated, is of personal importance to Him. The reaction of the divine self (Amos 6:8; Jer. 5:9; 51:14), its manifestations in the form of love, mercy, disappointment, or anger convey the profound intensity of the divine inwardness.

PROPHETIC REFLECTION BEGINS, we might say, with the abuse and consequent failure of freedom, with the irrationality of human conduct, and it points to God who stands above history. Man-made history is not history's only dimension. The pathos and judgment of God transcend the human dimension. Great conquerors are seen as mere tools of His mysterious will. Man has choice, but not sovereignty.

History is not a meaningless conglomeration of neutral facts, but a drama unfolding the relationship between God and man. The drama is staged in time and encompasses the wide arena of human affairs. A battle is raging: man in his presumption undertakes to fashion history in disregard and defiance of God. The prophets witness the misery that man endures as well as man's wickedness that God endures, and even tolerates.

But God is wrestling with man. History is where God is defied, where His judgment is enacted, and where His kingship is to be established. For it is of the realm of space, not of the realm of history, that the seraphim proclaim: "It is full of His glory." Only a sprinkling of His glory is found in history.

THE THEOLOGY OF PATHOS brings about a shift in the understanding of man's ultimate problems. The prophet does not see the human situation in and of itself. The predicament of man is the predicament of God, who has a stake in the human situation. Sin, guilt, suffering cannot be separated from the divine situation. The life of sin is more than a failure of man; it is a frustration to God. Thus, man's alienation from God is not the ultimate fact by which to measure man's situation. The divine pathos, the fact of God's participation in the predicament of man, is the elemental fact.

The essential meaning of pathos is, therefore, not to be seen in its psychological denotation, as standing for a state of the soul, but in its theological connotation, signifying God as involved in history. He is engaged to Israel – and has a stake in its destiny. The profundity of this insight can be sensed only in the light of the prophets' awareness of the mystery and transcendence of God. For the biblical understanding of history, the idea of pathos is as central as the idea of man being an image of God is for the understanding of creation.

The biblical writers were aware of the paradox involved in God's relation to man. "Behold, to the Lord your God belong heaven and the heaven of heavens, the earth with all that is in it; yet the Lord set His heart in love upon your fathers and chose their descendants after them, you above all peoples, as at this day" (Deut. 10:14–15).

Never in history has man been taken as seriously as in prophetic thinking. Man is not only an image of God; he is a perpetual concern of God. The idea of pathos adds a new dimension to human existence. Whatever man does affects not only his own life, but also the life of God insofar as it is directed to man. The import of man raises him beyond the level of mere creature. He is a consort, a partner, a factor in the life of God.

OUR EMBARRASSMENT in reading the harsh expressions of divine wrath is also due to the general disposition of modern man. We have no sense for spiritual grandeur. Spiritual to us means ethereal, calm, moderate, slight, imperceptible. We respond to beauty;

grandeur is unbearable. We are moved by a soft religiosity, and would like to think that God is lovely, tender,
and familiar, as if faith were a source of comfort, but not
readiness for martyrdom.

To our mind the terrible threats of castigation
bespeak a lack of moderation. Is it not because we are
only dimly aware of the full gravity of human failure,
of the sufferings inflicted by those who revile God's
demand for justice? There is a cruelty which pardons,
just as there is a pity which punishes. Severity must tame
those whom love cannot win.

Those of us to whom the crimes of the world are mere
incidents, and the agony of the poor is one of the many
facts of life, may be inclined to describe the God of the
prophets as stern, arbitrary, inscrutable, even unaccount-
able. But the thought of God and indifference to other
people's suffering are mutually exclusive.

Nothing is so sweet to the heart of man as love.
However, for love to function, the suppression of sympathy may be necessary. A surgeon would be a failure
if he indulged his natural sympathy at the sight of a
bleeding wound. He must suppress his emotion to save a
life, he must hurt in order to heal. Genuine love, genuine
mercy, must not be taken to be indulgence of mere

feeling, excess of sensibility, which is commonly called sentimentality.

No single attribute can convey the nature of God's relationship to man. Since justice is His nature, love, which would disregard the evil deeds of man, would contradict His nature. Because of His concern for man, His justice is tempered with mercy. Divine anger is not the antithesis of love, but its counterpart, a help to justice as demanded by true love.

The end of sentimentality is the enfeeblement of truth and justice. It is divine anger that gives strength to God's truth and justice. There are moments in history when anger alone can conquer evil. It is after mildness and kindness have failed that anger is proclaimed.

EVEN MORE FRUSTRATING than the fact that evil is real, mighty, and tempting is the fact that it thrives so well in the disguise of the good, that it can draw its nutriment from the life of the holy. In this world, it seems, the holy and the unholy do not exist apart, but are mixed, interrelated, and confounded. It is a world where idols may be rich in beauty, and where the worship of God may be tinged with wickedness.

It was not the lack of religion but the perversion of it that the prophets of Israel denounced. "Many an altar has Ephraim raised, altars that only serve for sin" (Hos. 8:11). "The priests said not: Where is the Lord? And they that handle the law knew Me not" (Jer. 2:8). The greater the man, the more he is exposed to sin. Piety is at times evil in disguise, an instrument in the pursuit of power.

AND YET THERE IS SOMETHING in the world that the Bible does regard as a symbol of God. It is not a temple nor a tree, it is not a statue nor a star. The symbol of God is *man, every man*. God created man in His image (*tselem*), in His likeness (*demuth*). How significant is the fact that the term *tselem*, which is frequently used in a damnatory sense for a man-made image of God, as well as the term *demuth* – of which Isaiah claims (40:18), no *demuth* or likeness can be applied to God – are employed in denoting man as an image and likeness of God.

Human life is holy, holier even than the scrolls of the Torah. Its holiness is not man's achievement; it is a gift of God rather than attained through merit. Man must, therefore, be treated with the honor due to a likeness representing the King of kings.

41

Not that the Bible was unaware of man's frailty and wickedness. The divine in man is not by virtue of what he does but by virtue of what he is. With supreme frankness the failures and shortcomings of kings and prophets, of men such as Moses or David, are recorded. And yet, biblical tradition insists that not only man's soul but also his body is symbolic of God. This is why even the body of a criminal condemned to death must be treated with reverence, according to the book of Deuteronomy (21:23). He who sheds the blood of a human being, "it is accounted to him as though he diminished or destroyed the divine image" (Mekilta to Exodus 20:16). . . .

Since not one man or one particular nation but all people of all nations are endowed the likeness of God, there is no danger of ever worshipping man, because only that which is extraordinary and different may become an object of worship. But the divine likeness is something all people share.

This is a conception of far-reaching importance to biblical piety. What it implies can hardly be summarized. Reverence for God is shown in our reverence for man. The fear you must feel of offending or hurting a human being must be as ultimate as your fear of God. An act of violence is an act of desecration. To be arrogant toward man is to be blasphemous toward God. . . .

The divine symbolism of man is not in what he *has* – such as reason or the power of speech – but in what he *is* potentially: he is able to be holy as God is holy. To imitate God, to act as He acts in mercy and love, is the way of enhancing our likeness. Man becomes what he worships. "Says the Holy One, blessed be He: He who acts like Me shall be like Me." Says Rabbi Levi ben Hama: "Idolaters resemble their idols (Psalms 115:8); now how much more must the servants of the Lord resemble Him" (Deuteronomy Rabba 1:10).

And yet that likeness may be defiled, distorted, and forfeited. It is from the context of this problem that the entire issue of Jewish symbolism must be considered. The goal of man is to recognize and preserve his likeness or at least to prevent its distortion.

But man has failed. And what is the consequence? "I have placed the likeness of My image on them and through their sins I have upset it," is the dictum of God (Moed Katan 15b).

The likeness is all but gone. Today, nothing is more remote and less plausible than the idea that man is a symbol of God. Man forgot Whom he represents or *that* he represents.

There is one hope. The Midrash interprets the verse Deuteronomy 1:10, as if it were written: Lo, today you are like the stars in heaven, but in the future you will resemble the Master. (Deuteronomy Rabba 1:10).

The likeness of God is broken, yet not utterly destroyed.

5

God Demands Justice

IN A SENSE, the calling of the prophet may be described as that of an advocate or champion, speaking for those who are too weak to plead their own cause. Indeed, the major activity of the prophets was *interference*, remonstrating about wrongs inflicted on other people, meddling in affairs which were seemingly neither their concern nor their responsibility. A prudent man is he who minds his own business, staying away from questions which do not involve his own interests, particularly when not authorized to step in – and prophets were given no mandate by the widows and orphans to plead their cause. The prophet is a person who is not tolerant of the wrongs done to others, who resents other people's injuries.

WHY SHOULD RELIGION, the essence of which is worship of God, put such stress on justice for man? Does not the preoccupation with morality tend to divest religion of immediate devotion to God? Why should a worldly virtue like justice be so important to the Holy One of Israel? Did not the prophets overrate the worth of justice?

Perhaps the answer lies here: righteousness is not just a value; it is God's part of human life, *God's stake in human history.* Perhaps it is because the suffering of man is a blot upon God's conscience; because it is in relations between man and man that God is at stake. Or is it simply because the infamy of a wicked act is infinitely greater than we are able to imagine? People act as they please, doing what is vile, abusing the weak, not realizing that they are fighting God, affronting the divine, or that the oppression of man is a humiliation of God.

> *He who oppresses a poor man insults his Maker,*
> *He who is kind to the needy honors Him.*
>
> (Prov. 14:31; cf. 17:5)

The universe is done. The greater masterpiece still undone, still in the process of being created, is history. For accomplishing His grand design, God needs the help of man. Man is and has the instrument of God, which he may or may not use in consonance with the grand design. Life is clay, and righteousness the mold in which God wants history to be shaped. But human beings, instead of fashioning the clay, deform the shape.

The world is full of iniquity, of injustice and idolatry. The people offer animals; the priests offer incense. But God needs mercy, righteousness; His needs cannot be satisfied in the temples, in space, but only in history, in time. It is within the realm of history that man is charged with God's mission.

Justice is not an ancient custom, a human convention, a value, but a transcendent demand, freighted with divine concern. It is not only a relationship between man and man, it is an *act* involving God, a divine need. Justice is His line, righteousness His plummet (Isa. 28:17). It is not one of His ways, but in all His ways. Its validity is not only universal, but also eternal, independent of will and experience.

People think that to be just is a virtue, deserving honor and rewards; that in doing righteousness one confers a favor on society. No one expects to receive a reward for the habit of breathing. Justice is as much a necessity as breathing is, and a constant occupation.

THE PREOCCUPATION WITH JUSTICE, the passion with which the prophets condemn injustice, is rooted in their sympathy with divine pathos. The chief characteristic of prophetic thought is the primacy of God's involvement in history. History is the domain with which the prophets' minds are occupied. They are moved by a responsibility for society, by a sensitivity to what the moment demands.

Since the prophets do not speak in the name of the moral law, it is inaccurate to characterize them as proclaimers of justice, or *mishpat*. It is more accurate to see them as proclaimers of God's pathos, speaking not for the idea of justice, but for the God of justice, for God's concern for justice. Divine concern remembered in sympathy is the stuff of which prophecy is made.

To the biblical mind the implication of goodness is mercy. Pathos, concern for the world, is the very ethos of God. This ethical sensitivity of God – not the ethical in and for itself – is reflected in the prophets' declarations. Prophetic morality rests upon both a divine command

and a divine concern. Its ultimate appeal is not to the reasonableness of the moral law, but to the fact that God has demanded it and that its fulfillment is a realization of His concern.

THE PROPHET IS A MAN who feels fiercely. God has thrust a burden upon his soul, and he is bowed and stunned at man's fierce greed. Frightful is the agony of man; no human voice can convey its full terror. Prophecy is the voice that God has lent to the silent agony, a voice to the plundered poor, to the profaned riches of the world. It is a form of living, a crossing point of God and man. God is raging in the prophets' words. . . .

Tranquility is unknown to the soul of a prophet. The miseries of the world give him no rest. While others are callous, and even callous to their callousness and unaware of their insensitivity, the prophets remain examples of supreme impatience with evil, distracted by neither might nor applause, by neither success nor beauty. Their intense sensitivity to right and wrong is due to their intense sensitivity to God's concern for right and wrong. They feel fiercely because they hear deeply.

The weakness of many systems of moral philosophy is in their isolationism. The isolation of morality is an assumption that the good is unrelated to the morally neutral values. However, there is an interrelatedness between the moral and all other acts of man, whether in the realm of theory or in the realm of aesthetic or technical application, and the moral person must not be thought of as if he were a professional magician, moral in some situations and immoral in others.

Consequently, the moral problem cannot be solved as a moral problem. It must be dealt with as part of the total issue of man. The supreme problem is all of life, not good and evil. We cannot deal with morality unless we deal with all of man, the nature of existence, of doing, of meaning.

The prophets tried to overcome the isolationism of religion. It is the prophets who teach us that the problem of living does not arise with the question of how to take care of the rascals, of how to prevent delinquency or hideous crimes. The problem of living begins with the realization of how we all blunder in dealing with our fellow men. The silent atrocities, the secret scandals, which no law can prevent, are the true seat of moral infection. The problem of living begins, in fact, in relation to our own selves, in the handling of our emotional functions, in the way we deal with envy, greed, and pride. What is first at stake in the life of man is not the fact of sin, of the wrong and corrupt, but the neutral acts, the needs. Our possessions pose no less a problem than our passions. The primary task, therefore, is not how to deal with the evil, but how to deal with the neutral, how to deal with needs.

Editor's note: The following passages specifically address the American civil rights movement. While the terminology may be dated, the issues are not.

WHAT IS AN IDOL? *Any god who is mine but not yours,* any god concerned with me but not with you, *is an idol.*

Faith in God is not simply *an afterlife–insurance policy. Racial or religious bigotry* must be recognized for what it is: *satanism, blasphemy.*

THE REDEEMING QUALITY of man lies in his ability to sense his kinship with all men. Yet there is a deadly poison that inflames the eye, making us see the generality of race but not the uniqueness of the human face. Pigmentation is what counts. The Negro is a stranger to many souls. There are people in our country whose moral sensitivity suffers a blackout when confronted with the black man's predicament.

THERE IS A FORM OF OPPRESSION which is more painful and more scathing than physical injury or economic privation. It is *public humiliation*. What afflicts my conscience is that my face, whose skin happens not to be dark, instead of radiating the likeness of God, has come to be taken as an image of haughty assumption and overbearance. Whether justified or not, I, the white man, have become in the eyes of others a symbol of arrogance and pretension, giving offense to other human beings, hurting their pride, even without intending it. My very presence inflicting insult!

THERE IS AN EVIL which most of us condone and are even guilty of: *indifference to evil.* We remain neutral, impartial, and not easily moved by the wrongs done unto other people. Indifference to evil is more insidious than evil itself; it is more universal, more contagious, more dangerous. A silent justification, it makes possible an evil erupting as an exception becoming the rule and being in turn accepted.

The prophets' great contribution to humanity was the discovery of *the evil of indifference.* One may be decent and sinister, pious and sinful.

The prophet is a person who suffers the harms done to others. Wherever a crime is committed, it is as if the prophet were the victim and the prey. The prophet's angry words cry. The wrath of God is a lamentation. All prophecy is one great exclamation: God is not indifferent to evil! He is always concerned, He is personally affected by what man does to man. He is a God of pathos.

In condemning the clergymen who joined Dr. Martin Luther King Jr. in protesting against local statutes and practices which denied constitutional liberties to groups of citizens on account of race, a white preacher declared: "The job of the minister is to lead the souls of men to God, not to bring about confusion by getting tangled up in transitory social problems."

In contrast to this definition, the prophets passionately proclaim that God himself is concerned with "the transitory social problems," with the blights of society, with the affairs of the marketplace.

What is the essence of being a prophet? *A prophet is a person who holds God and men in one thought at one time, at all times.* Our tragedy begins with *the segregation of God*, with the bifurcation of the secular and sacred. We worry more about the purity of dogma than about the *integrity of love. We think of God in the past tense* and refuse to realize that *God is always present* and *never, never past*; that God may be more intimately p*resent in slums than in mansions, with those who are smarting under the abuse of the callous.*

There are, of course, many among us whose record in dealing with the Negroes and other minority groups is unspotted. However, an honest estimation of the moral state of our society will disclose: *Some are guilty, but all are responsible.* If we admit that the individual is in some measure conditioned or affected by the public climate of opinion, an individual's crime discloses society's corruption. In a community not indifferent to suffering, uncompromisingly impatient with cruelty and falsehood, racial discrimination would be infrequent rather than common.

That equality is a good thing, a fine goal, may be generally accepted. What is lacking is a sense of the *monstrosity of inequality.* Seen from the perspective of prophetic faith, the predicament of justice is the predicament of God.

Of course, more and more people are becoming aware of the Negro problem, but they fail to grasp its being a personal problem. People are increasingly fearful of social tension and disturbance. However, so long as our society is more concerned to prevent racial strife than to prevent humiliation, the cause of strife, its moral status will be depressing, indeed.

6

Modernity Has Forfeited the Spirit

TECHNICAL CIVILIZATION is man's conquest of space. It is a triumph frequently achieved by sacrificing an essential ingredient of existence, namely, time. In technical civilization, we expend time to gain space. To enhance our power in the world of space is our main objective. Yet to have more does not mean to be more. The power we attain in the world of space terminates abruptly at the borderline of time. But time is the heart of existence.

To gain control of the world of space is certainly one of our tasks. The danger begins when in gaining power in the realm of space we forfeit all aspirations in the realm of time. There is a realm of time where the goal is not to have but to be, not to own but to give, not to control but to share, not to subdue but to be in accord. Life goes wrong when the control of space, the acquisition of things of space, becomes our sole concern.

Nothing is more useful than power, nothing more frightful. We have often suffered from degradation by poverty; now we are threatened with degradation through power. There is happiness in the love of labor; there is misery in the love of gain. Many hearts and pitchers are broken at the fountain of profit. Selling himself into slavery to things, man becomes a utensil that is broken at the fountain.

AS CIVILIZATION ADVANCES, the sense of wonder almost necessarily declines. Such decline is an alarming symptom of our state of mind. Mankind will not perish for want of information, but only for want of appreciation. The beginning of our happiness lies in the understanding that life without wonder is not worth living. What we lack is not a will to believe but a will to wonder.

OUR AGE IS ONE in which usefulness is thought to be the chief merit of nature; in which the attainment of power, the utilization of its resources, is taken to be the chief purpose of man in God's creation. Man has indeed become primarily a tool-making animal, and the world is now a gigantic toolbox for the satisfaction of his needs.

The Greeks learned in order to comprehend. The Hebrews learned in order to revere. The modern man learns in order to use. To Bacon we owe the formulation, "Knowledge is power." This is how people are urged to study: knowledge means success. We do not know anymore how to justify any value except in terms of expediency. Man is willing to define himself as "a seeker after the maximum degree of comfort for the minimum expenditure of energy." He equates value with that which avails. He feels, acts, and thinks as if the sole purpose of the universe were to satisfy his needs. To the modern man everything seems calculable; everything reducible to a figure. He has supreme faith in statistics and abhors the idea of a mystery. Obstinately he ignores the fact that we are all surrounded by things which we apprehend but cannot comprehend; that even reason is a mystery to itself. He is sure of his ability to explain all mystery away. Only a generation ago he was convinced that science was on the way to solve all the enigmas of the world. In the words of a poet:

Whatever there is to know
That we shall know some day.

Religious knowledge is regarded as the lowest form of knowledge. The human mind, according to Comte, goes through three stages of thought: the theological, the metaphysical, and the positive. Out of the primitive religious knowledge metaphysics gradually evolved, to be succeeded by the positive, scientific method of thought. Modern man, having achieved the final stage, eschews all appeal to unobservable entities. In the place of God, humanity – the *grand Être* – becomes the supreme object of adoration. However, what is considered an achievement from the perspective of modern man may be judged a privation by the postmodern man. . . .

Dazzled by the brilliant achievements of the intellect in science and technique, we have not only become convinced that we are the masters of the earth; we have become convinced that our needs and interests are the ultimate standard of what is right and wrong.

Comfort, luxuries, success continually bait our appetite, impairing our vision of that which is required but not always desired. They make it easy for us to grow blind to values. Interests are the value-blind man's dog, his pathfinder and his guide.

MODERN MAN is gradually recovering from the shock of realizing that, intellectually, he has no right to dream anymore; no right to mourn his lost craving for that which he may need but to which he has become indifferent. He has, indeed, long since ceased to trust his will to believe or even his grief about the loss of a desire to believe.

A shudder stalks through our nights. There is no house in our cities without at least one soul wailing in the midst of joy, terrified by achievement, dismayed at the servitude to needs, at the inability to trust what he is cherishing.

What applies to moral judgments holds true in regard to religious beliefs. It has long been known that need and desire play a part in the shaping of beliefs. But is it true, as modern psychology often claims, that our religious beliefs are nothing but attempts to satisfy subconscious wishes? That the conception of God is merely a projection of self-seeking emotions, an objectification of subjective needs, the self in disguise? Indeed, the tendency to question the genuineness of man's concern about God is a challenge no less serious than the tendency to question the existence of God. We are in greater need of a proof for the authenticity of faith than of a proof for the existence of God.

We have not only forfeited faith; we have lost our faith in the meaning of faith. All we have is a sense of horror. We are afraid of man. We are terrified at our own power. Our proud Western civilization has not withstood the stream of cruelty and crime that burst forth out of the undercurrents of evil in the human soul. We nearly drown in a stream of guilt and misery that leaves no conscience clean. What have we done with our power? What have we done to the world? The flood of wretchedness is sweeping away our monstrous conceit. Who is the Lord? We despair of ever regaining an awareness of Him, of ever regaining faith in the meaning of faith. Indeed, out of a system of ideas where knowledge is power, where values are a synonym for needs, where the pyramid of being is turned upside down – it is hard to find a way to an awareness of God. If the world is only power to us and we are all absorbed in a gold rush, then the only god we may come upon is the golden calf. Nature as a toolbox is a world that does not point beyond itself. It is when nature is sensed as mystery and grandeur that it calls upon us to look beyond it.

The awareness of grandeur and the sublime is all but gone from the modern mind. Our systems of education stress the importance of enabling the student to exploit the power aspect of reality. To some degree, they try to develop his ability to appreciate beauty. But there is no education for the sublime. We teach the children how to measure, how to weigh. We fail to teach them how to revere, how to sense wonder and awe. The sense for the sublime, the sign of the inward greatness of the human soul and something which is potentially given to all people, is now a rare gift. Yet without it, the world becomes flat and the soul a vacuum. Here is where the biblical view of reality may serve us as a guide. Significantly, the theme of biblical poetry is not the charm or beauty of nature; it is the grandeur, it is the *sublime* aspect of nature which biblical poetry is trying to celebrate.

THE BIBLE DOES NOT CLAIM that things speak to man; it only claims that things speak to God. Inanimate objects are dead in relation to man; they are alive in relation to God. They sing to God. The mountains melt like wax, the waters tremble at the presence of the Lord (Pss. 77:17; 97:5). "Tremble, O earth, at the presence of the Lord, at the presence of the God of Jacob" (Ps. 114:7).

Whose ear has heard the trees sing to God? Has our reason ever thought of calling upon the sun to praise the Lord? And yet, what the ear fails to perceive, what reason fails to conceive, the Bible makes clear to our souls. It is a higher truth, to be grasped by the spirit.

Modern man dwells upon the order and power of nature; the prophets dwell upon the grandeur and creation of nature. The former directs his attention to the manageable and intelligible aspect of the universe; the latter to its mystery and marvel. What the prophets sense in nature is not a direct reflection of God but an allusion to Him. Nature is not a part of God but rather a fulfillment of His will.

"Lift up your eyes on high and see who created these" (Isa. 40:26). There is a higher form of seeing. We must learn how to lift up our eyes on high in order to see that the world is more a question than an answer. The world's beauty and power are as naught compared to Him. The grandeur of nature is only the beginning. *Beyond the grandeur is God.*

The biblical man does not see nature in isolation but in relation to God. "At the beginning God created heaven and earth" – these few words set forth the contingency and absolute dependence of all of reality. What, then, is reality? To the Western man, it is *a thing in itself*; to the biblical man, it is *a thing through God*. Looking at a thing the biblical man's eyes see not so much form, color, force, and motion as an act of God. The world is a gate, not a wall.

THE UNDERLYING ASSUMPTION of modern man's outlook is that objective reality is physical: all non-material phenomena can be reduced to material phenomena and explained in physical terms. Thus, only those types of human experiences which acquaint us with the quantitative aspects of material phenomena refer to the real world. None of the other types of our experience, such as prayer or the awareness of the presence of God, has any objective counterpart. They are illusory in the sense that they do not acquaint us with the nature of the objective world.

In modern society, he who refuses to accept the equation of the real and the physical is considered a mystic. However, since God is not an object of a physical experience, the equation implies the impossibility of His existence. Either God is but a word not designating anything real or He is at least as real as the man I see in front of me.

This is the premise of faith: Spiritual events are real. Ultimately, all creative events are caused by spiritual acts. The God who creates heaven and earth is the God who communicates His will to the mind of man.

THE MOST SERIOUS OBSTACLE which modern men encounter in entering a discussion about revelation does not arise from their doubts as to whether the accounts of the prophets about their experiences are authentic. The most critical vindication of these accounts, even if it were possible, would be of little relevance. The most serious problem is *the absence of the problem*. An answer, to be meaningful, presupposes the awareness of a question, but the climate in which we live today is not congenial to the continued growth of questions which have taken centuries to cultivate. The Bible is an answer to the supreme question: *What does God demand of us?* Yet the question has gone out of the world. God is portrayed as a mass of vagueness behind a veil of enigmas, and His voice has become alien to our minds, to our hearts, to our souls. We have learned to listen to every "I" except the "I" of God. The man of our time may proudly declare: nothing animal is alien to me but everything divine is. This is the status of the Bible in modern life: it is a sublime answer, but we do not know the question anymore. Unless we recover the question, there is no hope of understanding the Bible.

IT MAY SEEM EASY to play with the idea that the Bible is a book like many other books, or that the story of Sinai is a fairy tale. Yet it is in such playing that we may gamble away our commitment, our tie to God.

Consider what such denial implies. If Moses and Isaiah have failed to find out what the will of God is, who will? If God is not found in the Bible, where should we seek Him?

The question about the Bible is the question about the world. It is an ultimate question. If God had nothing to do with the prophets, then He has nothing to do with mankind. And if God had anything to do with the prophets, then the prophets were neither liars nor impostors.

And yet, we, Philistines, continue to insist upon intellectual clichés, upon setting up our own life as a model and measure of what prophets could possibly

attain. We oppose the prophets' word with our claims
that God can never reach an ear, God will never stoop to
light a word in the mind of man. But this is the principle
of fools: what is unattainable to us is unattainable
to others. The average man is not the measure. It is
not an achievement of man that we are exploring. It
is something in which the power of God was active.
It is not for us to say that God must conform to our
standards. The platitudes of our theories must not
decide the greatest issue. There are many things between
God and man of which scholars have never dreamt.
Does psychology decide the validity of mathematical
laws? Does history proceed the way logic predicts?

7

Prayer Is Being Known by God

PRAYER IS NOT THINKING. To the thinker, God is an object; to the man who prays, He is the subject. Awaking in the presence of God, we strive not to acquire an objective knowledge, but to deepen the mutual allegiance of man and God. What we want is not to know Him, but to be known to Him; not to form judgments about Him, but to be judged by Him; not to make the world an object of our mind, but to let the world come to His attention, to augment His, rather than our, knowledge. We endeavor to disclose ourselves to the Sustainer of all, rather than to enclose the world in ourselves.

FOR NEITHER THE LIPS nor the brain are the limits of the scene in which prayer takes place. Speech and devotion are functions auxiliary to a metaphysical process. Common to all men who pray is the certainty that prayer is an act which makes the heart audible to God. Who would pour his most precious hopes into an abyss? Essential is the metaphysical rather than the physical dimension of prayer. Prayer is not a thought that rambles alone in the world, but an event that starts in man and ends in God. What goes on in our heart is a humble preliminary to an event in God.

ULTIMATELY, THE GOAL of prayer is not to translate a word but to translate the self; not to render an ancient vocabulary in modern terminology, but to transform our thoughts into thoughts of prayer. Prayer is the soul's *imitation of the spirit*, of the spirit that is contained in the liturgical words.

WHAT, AS A RULE, makes it possible for us to pray is our ability to affiliate our own minds with the pattern of fixed texts, to unlock our hearts to the words, and to surrender to their meanings. The words stand before us as living entities full of spiritual power, of a power which often surpasses the grasp of our minds. The words are often the givers, and we the recipients. They inspire our minds and awaken our hearts.

Most of us do not know the answer to one of the most important questions, namely, What is our ultimate concern? We do not know what to pray for. It is the liturgy that teaches us what to pray for. It is through the words of the liturgy that we discover what moves us unawares, what is urgent in our lives, what in us is related to the ultimate.

We do not realize how much we acquire by dwelling upon the treasures of the liturgy until we learn how to commune with the spirit of Israel's prophets and saints. It is more inspiring to let the heart echo the music of the ages than to play upon the broken flutes of our own hearts. . . .

It is good that there are words sanctified by ages of worship, by the honesty and love of generations. If it were left to ourselves, who would know what word is right to be offered as praise in the sight of God or which of our perishable thoughts is worthy of entering eternity?

PRAYER IS THE MICROCOSM of the soul. It is the whole soul in one moment; the quintessence of all our acts; the climax of all our thoughts. It rises as high as our thoughts. Now, if the Torah is nothing but the national literature of the Jewish people, if the mystery of revelation is discarded as superstition, then prayer is hardly more than a soliloquy. If God does not have power to speak to us, how should we possess the power to speak to Him? Thus, prayer is a part of a greater issue. It depends upon the total spiritual situation of man and upon a mind within which God is at home. Of course, if our lives are too barren to bring forth the spirit of worship; if all our thoughts and anxieties do not contain enough spiritual substance to be distilled into prayer, an inner transformation is a matter of emergency. And such an emergency we face today. *The issue of prayer is not prayer; the issue of prayer is God.* One cannot pray unless one has faith in one's own ability to accost the infinite, merciful, eternal God.

Moreover, we must not overlook one of the profound principles of Judaism. There is something which is far greater than my desire to pray, namely, God's desire that

I pray. There is something which is far greater than my will to believe, namely, God's will that I believe. How insignificant is the outpouring of my soul in the midst of this great universe! Unless it is the will of God that I pray, unless God desires our prayer, how ludicrous is all my praying.

We cannot reach heaven by building a Tower of Babel. The biblical way *to* God is a way *of* God. God's waiting for our prayers is that which lends meaning to them.

8

A Pattern for Living

WE ARE OFTEN INCLINED to define the essence of religion as a state of the soul, as inwardness, as an absolute feeling, and expect a person who is religious to be endowed with a kind of sentiment too deep to rise to the surface of common deeds, as if religion were a plant that can only thrive at the bottom of the ocean. As we have seen, religion is not a feeling for something that is, but an answer to Him who is asking us to live in a certain way. It is in its very origin a consciousness of duty, of being committed to higher ends; a realization that life is not only man's but also God's sphere of interest.

Faith does not come to an end with attaining certainty of His existence. Faith is the beginning of intense craving to enter a synthesis with Him who is beyond the mystery, to bring together all the might that is within us with all that is spiritual beyond us. At the root of our yearning for integrity is a stir of the inexpressible within us to commune with the ineffable beyond us. But what is the language of that communion, without which our impulse remains inarticulate?

We are taught that what God asks of man is more than an inner attitude, that He gives man not only life but also a law, that His will is to be served not only adored, obeyed not only worshipped. Faith comes over us like a force urging for action, to which we respond by pledging ourselves to constancy of devotion, committing us to the presence of God, and remains an affiliation for life, an allegiance involving restraint, submission, self-control, and courage.

. . . As faith cannot exist without a creed, piety cannot subsist without a pattern of deeds; as intelligence cannot be separated from training, religion cannot be divorced from conduct. Judaism is lived in deeds, not only in thoughts.

A pattern for living – the object of man's most urgent quest – which would correspond to his dignity, must take into consideration not only his ability to exploit the forces of nature and to appreciate the loveliness of its forms, but also his unique sense of the ineffable. It must be a design, not only for the satisfaction of needs, but also for the attainment of ends.

THE QUEST FOR RIGHT LIVING, the question of what is to be done right now, right here, is the authentic core of Jewish religion. It has been the main theme of Jewish literature, from the prophets till the times of the Hasidim, and it has been explored with a sense of urgency, as if life were a continuous state of emergency.

With quiet sadness and rich with strenuous lessons of defeat, we learn today to understand that there are no extemporaneous solutions to perpetual problems; that the only safeguard against constant danger is constant vigilance, constant guidance. Such guidance, such vigilance is given to him who lives in the shadows of Sinai, whose weeks, days, hours are set in the rhythm of the Torah.

What constitutes the Jewish form of living is not so much the performance of single good deeds, the taking of a step now and then, as the pursuit of a way, being on the way; not so much the acts of fulfilling as the state of being committed to the task, of belonging to an order in which single deeds, aggregates of religious feeling, sporadic sentiments, moral episodes become parts of a complete pattern.

PSYCHIC LIFE, too, is a constant process of growth and waste, and its needs cannot be satisfied by scanty, desultory injections. Not being a hibernating animal, man cannot live by what he stores away. He may have a full memory and an empty soul. Unfree men are horrified by the suggestion of accepting a spiritual regimen. Associating inner control with external tyranny, they would rather suffer than be subject to spiritual authority. Only free men, those who are not prone to canonize every caprice, do not equate self-restraint with self-surrender, knowing that no man is free who is not a master of himself, that the more liberties we enjoy, the more discipline we need.

JUDAISM TEACHES US how even the gratification of animal needs can be an act of sanctification.

The enjoyment of food may be a way of purification. Something of my soul may be drowned in a glass of water, when its content is gulped down as if nothing in the world mattered except my thirst. But we can come a bit closer to God, when remembering Him still more in excitement and passion.

Sanctification is not an unearthly concept. There is no dualism of the earthly and the sublime. All things are sublime. They were all created by God and their continuous being, their blind adherence to the laws of necessity are a way of obedience to the Creator. The existence of things throughout the universe is a supreme ritual.

A man alive, a flower blooming in the spring, is a fulfillment of God's command: "Let there be!" In living we are directly doing the will of God, in a way which is beyond choice or decision. This is why our very existence is contact with His will, why life is holy and a responsibility of God as well as man."

JUDAISM IS A THEOLOGY of the common deed, of the trivialities of life, dealing not so much with the training for the exceptional as with the management of the trivial. The predominant feature in the Jewish pattern of life is unassuming, inconspicuous piety rather than extravagance, mortification, asceticism. Thus, the purpose seems to be to ennoble the common, to endow worldly things with hieratic beauty; to attune the comparative to the absolute, to associate the detail with the whole, to adapt our own being with its plurality, conflicts, and contradictions to the all-transcending unity, to the holy.

WORSHIP AND LIVING are not two separate realms. Unless living is a form of worship, our worship has no life. Religion is not a reservation, a tract of time reserved for solemn celebrations on festive days. The spirit withers when confined in splendid isolation. What is decisive is not the climax we reach in rare moments, but how the achievements of rare moments affect the climate of the entire life. The goal of Jewish law is to be the grammar of living, dealing with all relations and functions of living. Its main theme is the person rather than an institution.

Religion is not made for extraordinary occasions, such as birth, marriage, and death. Religion is trying to teach us that no act is trite, every moment is an extraordinary occasion.

A Pattern for Living

The highest peak of spiritual living is not necessarily reached in rare moments of ecstasy; the highest peak lies wherever we are and may be ascended in a common deed. There can be as sublime a holiness in performing friendship, in observing dietary laws day by day, as in uttering a prayer on the Day of Atonement.

It is not by the rare act of greatness that character is determined, but by everyday actions, by a constant effort to rend our callousness. It is constancy that sanctifies. Judaism is an attempt to place all of life under the glory of ultimate significance, to relate all scattered actions to the One. Through the constant rhythm of prayers, disciplines, reminders, joys, man is taught not to forfeit his grandeur.

TO THE VULGAR MIND, a deed consists of the self trying to exploit the non-self. To the pious man, a deed is an encounter of the human and the holy, of man's will and God's world. Both are hewn from the same rock and destined to be parts of one great mosaic.

There is no dichotomy between the happiness of man and the designs of God. To discover the absence of that dichotomy, to live that identity, is the true reward of religious living. God shares man's joy, if man is open to God's concern. The satisfaction of a human need is a dedication to a divine end.

The world is torn by conflicts, by folly, by hatred. Our task is to cleanse, to illumine, to repair. Every deed is either a clash or an aid in the effort of redemption. Man is not one with God, not even with his true self. Our task is to bring eternity into time, to clear in the wilderness a way, to make plain in the desert a highway for God.

A JEW IS ASKED to take a *leap of action*, rather than a *leap of thought*. He is asked to surpass his needs, to do more than he understands in order to understand more than he does. In carrying out the word of the Torah he is ushered into the presence of spiritual meaning. Through the ecstasy of deeds he learns to be certain of the hereness of God. Right living is a way to right thinking. . . . What commitments must precede the experience of such meaning? What convictions must persist to make such insights possible? Our way of living must be compatible with our essence as created in the likeness of God. We must beware lest our likeness be distorted and even forfeited. In our way of living we must remain true not only to our sense of power and beauty but also to our sense of the grandeur and mystery of existence. The true meaning of existence is disclosed in moments of living in the presence of God. The problem we face is: How can we live in a way which is in agreement with such convictions?

HOW SHOULD MAN, a being created in the likeness of God, live? What way of living is compatible with the grandeur and mystery of living? It is a problem which man has always been anxious to ignore. Upon the pavement of the Roman city of Timgat an inscription was found which reads: "To hunt, to bathe, to gamble, to laugh, that is to live." Judaism is a reminder of the grandeur and earnestness of living.

In what dimension of existence does man become aware of the grandeur and earnestness of living? What are the occasions in which he discovers the nature of his own self? The necessity to diagnose and to heal the condition of the soul? In the solitude of self-reflection the self may seem to be a fountain of beautiful thoughts and ideals. Yet thought may be a spell, and ideals may be worn like borrowed diadems.

It is in *deeds* that man becomes aware of what his life really is, of his power to harm and to hurt, to wreck and to ruin; of his ability to derive joy and to bestow it upon others; to relieve and to increase his own and other people's tensions. It is in the employment of his will, not in reflection, that he meets his own self as it is; not as he should like it to be. In his deeds man exposes his immanent as well as his suppressed desires, spelling even that which he cannot apprehend. What he may not dare to think, he often utters in deeds. The heart is revealed in deeds.

The deed is the test, the trial, and the risk. What we perform may seem slight, but the aftermath is immense. An individual's misdeed can be the beginning of a nation's disaster. The sun goes down, but the deeds go on. Darkness is over all we have done. If man were able to survey at a glance all he has done in the course of his life, what would he feel? He would be terrified at the extent of his own power. To bind all we have done to our conscience or to our mind would be like trying to tie a torrent to a reed. Even a single deed generates an endless set of effects, initiating more than the most powerful man is able to master or to predict. A single deed may place the lives of countless people in the chains of its unpredictable effects. All we own is a passing intention, but what comes about will outlive and surpass our power. Gazing soberly at the world man is often overcome with a fear of action, a fear that, without knowledge of God's ways, turns to despair.

WHAT OUGHT WE TO DO? How ought we to conduct our lives? These are basic questions of ethics. They are also questions of religion. Philosophy of religion must inquire: Why do we ask these questions? Are they meaningful? On what grounds do we state them? To ethics, these are man's questions, necessitated by the nature of human existence. To religion, these are God's questions, and our answer to them concerns not only man but God.

"What ought I to do?" is, according to Kant, the basic question in ethics. Ours, however, is a more radical, meta-ethical approach. The ethical question refers to particular deeds; the meta-ethical question refers to all deeds. It deals with doing as such; not only what ought we to do, but what is our right to act at all? We are endowed with the ability to conquer and to control the forces of nature. In exercising power, we submit to our will a world that we did not create, invading realms that do not belong to us. Are we the kings of the universe or mere pirates? By whose grace, by what right, do we exploit, consume, and enjoy the fruits of the trees, the blessings of the earth? Who is responsible for the power to exploit, for the privilege to consume?

It is not an academic problem but an issue we face at every moment. By the will alone man becomes the most destructive of all beings. This is our predicament: our power may become our undoing. We stand on a razor's edge. It is so easy to hurt, to destroy, to insult, to kill. Giving birth to one child is a mystery; bringing death to millions is but a skill. It is not quite within the power of the human will to generate life; it is quite within the power of the will to destroy life.

In the midst of such anxiety we are confronted with the claim of the Bible. The world is not all danger, and man is not alone. God endowed man with freedom, and He will share in our use of freedom. The earth is the Lord's, and God is in search of man. He endowed man with power to conquer the earth, and His honor is upon our faith. We abused His power, we betrayed His trust. We cannot expect Him to say, "Though thou betrayest me, yet will I trust in thee."

Man is responsible for His deeds, and God is responsible for man's responsibility. He who is a life-giver must be a lawgiver. He shares in our responsibility. He is waiting to enter our deeds through our loyalty to His law. He may become a partner to our deeds.

God and man have a task in common as well as a common and mutual responsibility. The ultimate embarrassment is not a problem of solitary man but an intimate problem for both God and man. What is at stake is the meaning of God's creation, not only the meaning of man's existence. Religion is not a concern for man alone but a plea of God and a claim of man, God's expectation and man's aspiration. It is not an effort solely for the sake of man. Religion spells a task within the world of man, but its ends go far beyond. This is why the Bible proclaimed a law not only for man but for both God and man.

9

The Deed Is Wiser than the Heart

THE CAUSE OF NEARLY ALL FAILURES in human relations is this – that while we admire and extol the tasks, we fail to acquire the tools. Neither the naked hand nor the soul left to itself can effect much. It is by instruments that work is done. The soul needs them as much as the hand. And as the instruments of the hand either give motion or guide it, so the instruments of the soul supply either suggestions or cautions. The meaningfulness of the mitzvoth [commandments] consists in their being vehicles by which we advance on the road to spiritual ends.

Faith is not a silent treasure to be kept in seclusion of the soul, but a mint in which to strike the coin of common deeds. It is not enough to be dedicated in the soul, to consecrate moments in the stillness of contemplation.

The dichotomy of faith and works which presented such an important problem in Christian theology was never a problem in Judaism. To us, the basic problem is neither what is the right action nor what is the right intention. The basic problem is: What is right living? And life is indivisible. The inner sphere is never isolated from outward activities. Deed and thought are bound into one. All a person thinks and feels enters everything he does, and all he does is involved in everything he thinks and feels.

Spiritual aspirations are doomed to failure when we try to cultivate deeds at the expense of thoughts or thoughts at the expense of deeds. Is it the artist's inner vision or his wrestling with the stone that brings about a work of sculpture? Right living is like a work of art, the product of a vision and of a wrestling with concrete situations.

Judaism is averse to generalities, averse to looking for meaning in life detached from doing, as if the meaning were a separate entity. Its tendency is to make ideas convertible into deeds, to interpret metaphysical insights as patterns for action, to endow the most sublime principles with bearing upon everyday conduct.

In its tradition, the abstract became concrete, the absolute historic. By enacting the holy on the stage of concrete living, we perceive our kinship with the divine, the presence of the divine. What cannot be grasped in reflection, we comprehend in deeds.

THE WORLD NEEDS MORE than the secret holiness of individual inwardness. It needs more than sacred sentiments and good intentions. God asks for the heart because He needs the lives. It is by lives that the world will be redeemed, by lives that beat in concordance with God, by deeds that outbeat the finite charity of the human heart.

Man's power of action is less vague than his power of intention. And an action has intrinsic meaning; its value to the world is independent of what it means to the person performing it. The act of giving food to a helpless child is meaningful regardless of whether or not the moral intention is present. God asks for the heart, and we must spell our answer in terms of deeds.

It would be a device of conceit, if not presumption, to insist that purity of heart is the exclusive test of piety. Perfect purity is something we rarely know how to obtain or how to retain. No one can claim to have purged all the dross even from his finest desire. The self is finite, but selfishness is infinite.

God asks for the heart, but the heart is oppressed with uncertainty in its own twilight. God asks for faith, and the heart is not sure of its own faith. It is good that there is a dawn of decision for the night of the heart; deeds to objectify faith, definite forms to verify belief.

The heart is often a lonely voice in the marketplace of living. Man may entertain lofty ideals and behave like the ass that, as the saying goes, "carries gold and eats thistles." The problem of the soul is how to live nobly in an animal environment; how to persuade and train the tongue and the senses to behave in agreement with the insights of the soul.

The integrity of life is not exclusively a thing of the heart; it implies more than consciousness of the moral law. The innermost chamber must be guarded at the uttermost outposts. Religion is not the same as spiritualism; what man does in his concrete, physical existence is directly relevant to the divine. Spirituality is the goal, not the way of man. In this world music is played on physical instruments, and to the Jew the mitzvoth are the instruments on which the holy is carried out. If man were only mind, worship in thought would be the form in which to commune with God. But man is body and soul, and his goal is so to live that both "his heart and his flesh should sing to the living God."

WHERE IS THE PRESENCE, where is the glory of God to be found? It is found in the world ("the whole earth is full of His glory"), in the Bible, and in a sacred deed.

Do only the heavens declare the glory of God? It is deeply significant that Psalm 19 begins, "The heavens declare the glory of God," and concludes with a paean to the Torah and to the mitzvoth. The world, the word, as well as the sacred deed are full of His glory. God is more immediately found in the Bible as well as in acts of kindness and worship than in the mountains and forests. It is more meaningful for us to believe in the *immanence of God in deeds* than in the immanence of God in nature. Indeed, the concern of Judaism is primarily not how to find the presence of God in the world of things but how to let Him enter the ways in which we deal with things; how to be with Him in time, not only in space. This is why the mitzvah [good deed commanded by God] is a supreme source of religious insight and experience. The way to God is a way of God, and the mitzvah is a way of God, a way where the self-evidence of the Holy is disclosed. We have few words, but we know how to live in deeds that express God.

God is One, and His glory is One. And oneness means wholeness, indivisibility. His glory is not partly here and partly there; it is all here and all there. But here and now, in this world, the glory is concealed. It becomes revealed in a sacred deed, in a sacred moment, in a sacrificial deed. No one is lonely when doing a mitzvah, for a mitzvah is where God and man meet.

We do not meet Him in the way in which we meet things of space. To meet Him means to come upon an inner certainty of His realness, upon an awareness of His will. Such meeting, such presence, we experience in deeds.

"HOW CAN I REPAY unto the Lord all His bountiful dealings toward me?" (Ps. 116:12). How to answer the mystery that surrounds us, the ineffable that calls on our souls? This is, indeed, the universal theme of religion. The world is full of wonder. Who will answer? Who will care? Our reverence is no answer. The more deeply we revere the more clearly we realize the inadequacy of mere reverence. Is it enough to praise, to extol that which is beyond all praise? What is the worth of reverence? Faint are all our songs and praises. If we could only give away all we have, all we are. The only answer to the ineffable is a mode of living compatible with the ineffable.

Human life is a point where mind and mystery meet. This is why man cannot live by his reason alone, nor can he thrive on mystery alone. To surrender to the mystery is fatalism, to withdraw into reason is solipsism. Man is driven to commune with that which is beyond the mystery. The ineffable in him seeks a way to that which is beyond the ineffable.

Israel was taught how to accost Him who is beyond the mystery. Beyond the mind is mystery, but beyond the mystery is mercy. Out of the darkness comes a voice disclosing that the ultimate mystery is not an enigma but the God of mercy; that the Creator of all is the "Father in Heaven."

ANY RELIGIOUS OR ETHICAL teaching that places the main emphasis upon the virtues of inwardness such as faith and the purity of motivation must come to grief. If faith were the only standard, the effort of man would be doomed to failure. Indeed, the awareness of the weakness of the heart, the unreliability of human inwardness, may perhaps have been one of the reasons that compelled

Judaism to take recourse to actions instead of relying upon inward devotion. Perhaps this is the deeper meaning of the Rabbis' counsel: one should always do the good, even though it is not done for its own sake. It is the act that teaches us the meaning of the act.

The way to pure intention is paved with good deeds. The good is carried out in acts, and there is an intense fascination that comes from a good deed counteracting the pressure and ardor of the ego. The ego is redeemed by the absorbing power and the inexorable provocativeness of a just task which we face. It is the deed that carries us away, that transports the soul, proving to us that the greatest beauty grows at the greatest distance from the center of the ego.

Deeds set upon ideal goals, deeds performed not with careless ease and routine but in exertion and submission to their ends are stronger than the surprise and attack of caprice. Serving sacred goals may change mean motives. For such deeds are exacting. Whatever our motive may have been prior to the act, the act itself demands undivided attention. Thus the desire for reward is not the driving force of the poet in his creative moments, and the pursuit of pleasure or profit are not the essence of a religious or moral act.

At the moment in which an artist is absorbed in playing a concerto, the thought of applause, fame, or remuneration is far from his mind. His complete attention, his whole being is involved in the music. Should any extraneous thought enter his mind, it would arrest his concentration and mar the purity of his playing. The reward may have been on his mind when he negotiated with his agent, but during the performance it is the music that claims his complete concentration.

Man's situation in carrying out a religious or moral deed is similar. Left alone, the soul is subject to caprice. Yet there is power in the deed that purifies desires. It is the act, life itself, that educates the will. The good motive comes into being while doing the good.

If the initial motive is strong and pure, obtrusive intentions which emerge during the act may even serve to invigorate it, for the initial motive may absorb the vigor of the intruder into its own strength. Man may be replete with selfish motives but a deed and God are stronger than selfish motives. The redemptive power discharged in carrying out the good purifies the mind. The deed is wiser than the heart.

10

Something Is Asked of Us

HOW CAN WE BE SURE that oneness is really a way of God? How do we presume to know what is beyond the mystery? The certainty of being exposed to a presence not of the world is a fact of human existence. But such certainty does not find its fulfillment in esthetic contemplation; it is astir with a demand to live in a way that is worthy of that presence.

The beginning of faith is, as said above, not a feeling for the mystery of living or a sense of awe, wonder, and amazement. The root of religion is the question of what to do with the feeling for the mystery of living, what to do with awe, wonder, and amazement. Religion begins with the consciousness that something is asked of us. It is in that tense, eternal asking in which the soul is caught and in which man's answer is elicited.

Something is asked of us. But what? The ultimate question that stirs our soul is anonymous, mysterious, powerful, yet ineffable. Who will put into words, who will teach us the way of God? How shall we know that the way we choose is the way He wants us to pursue?

In moments of insight we are called to return. But how does one return? What is the way to Him? We all sense the grandeur and the mystery. But who will tell us how to answer the mystery? Who will tell us how to live in a way that is compatible with the grandeur, the mystery, and the glory? All we have is a perception but neither words nor deeds in which to phrase or to form an answer.

Man does not live by insight alone; he is in need of a creed, of dogma, of expression, of a way of living. Insights are not a secure possession; they are vague and sporadic. They are like divine sparks, flashing up before us and becoming obscure again, and we fall back into a darkness "almost as black as that in which we were before." The problem is: How to communicate those rare moments of insight to all hours of our life? How to commit intuition to concepts, the ineffable to words, insight to rational understanding? How to convey our insights to others and to unite in a fellowship of faith?

Moments of insight are not experienced with sufficient intensity by all people. Those sparks are powerful enough to light up a soul, but not enough to illumine the world. Has God never said, Let there be light, for all the world to see? In moments of insight God addresses himself to a single soul. Has He never addressed the world, a people, or a community? Has He left Himself without a trace in history for those who do not have the strength to seek Him constantly?

IN THINKING ABOUT THE WORLD, we cannot proceed without guidance, supplied by logic and scientific method. In thinking about the living God we must look to the prophets for guidance.

Those who share in the heritage of Israel believe that God is not always evasive. He confided Himself at rare moments to those who were chosen to be guides. We cannot express God, yet God expresses His will to us. It is through His word that we know that God is not beyond good and evil. Our own thinking would leave us in a state of bewilderment if it were not for the guidance we receive.

It is not right for us to be waiting for God, as if he had never entered history. In his quest for God, the man who lives after the age of Sinai must learn to understand the realness of God's search for man. He must not forget the prophets' world, God's waiting for man.

What a sculptor does to a block of marble, the Bible does to our finest intuitions. It is like raising the mystery to expression.

Private insights and inspirations prepare us to accept what the prophets convey. They enable us to understand the question to which revelation is an answer. For our faith does not derive its full substance from private insights. Our faith is faith by virtue of being a part of the community of Israel, by virtue of our having a share in the faith of prophets. From their words we derive the norms by which to test the veracity of our own insights.

It is through the prophets that we may be able to encounter Him as a Being who is beyond the mystery. In the prophets the ineffable became a voice, disclosing that God is not a being that is apart and away from ourselves, as ancient man believed, that He is not an enigma, but justice, mercy; not only a power to which we are accountable, but also a pattern for our lives. He is not the Unknown; He is the Father, the God of Abraham; out of the endless ages come compassion and guidance. Even the individual who feels forsaken remembers Him as the God of his fathers.

THE INDIVIDUAL'S INSIGHT alone is unable to cope with all the problems of living. It is the guidance of tradition on which we must rely, and whose norms we must learn to interpret and to apply. We must learn not only the ends but also the means by which to realize the ends; not only the general laws but also the particular forms.

Judaism calls upon us to listen *not only* to the voice of conscience but also the norms of heteronomous law. The good is not an abstract idea but a commandment, and the ultimate meaning of its fulfillment is in its being *an answer* to God.

THE DIVINE QUALITY of the Bible is not on display, it is not apparent to an inane, fatuous mind; just as the divine in the universe is not obvious to the debaucher. When we turn to the Bible with an empty spirit, moved by intellectual vanity, striving to show our superiority to the text; or as barren souls who go sightseeing to the words of the prophets, we discover the shells but miss the core. It is easier to enjoy beauty than to sense the holy. To be able to encounter the spirit within the words, we must learn to crave for an affinity with the pathos of God.

To sense the presence of God in the Bible, one must learn *to be present* to God in the Bible. Presence is not a concept, but a situation. To understand love it is not enough to read tales about it. One must be involved in the prophets to understand the prophets. One must be inspired to understand inspiration. Just as we cannot test thinking without thinking, we cannot sense holiness without being holy. Presence is not disclosed to those who are unattached and try to judge, to those who have no power to go beyond the values they cherish; to those who sense the story, not the pathos; the idea, not the realness of God.

The Bible is the frontier of the spirit where we must move and live in order to discover and to explore. It is open to him who gives himself to it, who lives with it intimately.

We can only sense the presence by being responsive to it. We must learn to respond before we may hear; we must learn to fulfill before we may know. *It is the Bible that enables us to know the Bible.* It is through the Bible that we discover what is in the Bible. Unless we are confronted with the word, unless we continue our dialogue with the prophets, unless we respond, the Bible ceases to be scripture.

We are moving in a circle. We would accept the Bible only if we could be sure of the presence of God in its words. Now, to identify His presence we must know what He is, but such knowledge we can only derive from the Bible. No human mind, conditioned as it is by its own perspectives, relations, and aspirations, is able, on its own, to proclaim for all people and all times, "This is God and nothing else." Thus we must accept the Bible in order to know the Bible; we must accept its unique authority in order to sense its unique quality. This, indeed, is the paradox of faith, the paradox of existence.

In our daily experience words are used as means to convey meaning. In the Bible to speak is to act, and the word is more than an instrument of expression; it is a vessel of divine power, the mystery of creation. The prophetic word creates, shapes, changes, builds, and destroys (see Jer. 1:10).

When man speaks, he tries to communicate some particular meaning; when the prophet speaks, he uncloses the source of all meaning. The words of the Bible are sources of spirit. They carry fire to the soul and evoke our lost dignity out of our hidden origins.

Illumined, we suddenly remember, we suddenly recover the strength of endless longing to sense eternity in time.

"He who prays speaks to God; but he who reads the Bible God speaks to him, as it is said (Ps. 119:99): 'Thy statutes are Thy converse with me'"(Yosippon).

II

Faith Is an Act of the Spirit

THINKING ABOUT GOD begins at the mind's rugged shore, where the murmur breaks off abruptly, where we do not know anymore how to yearn, how to be in awe. Only those who know how to live spiritually on edge will be able to go beyond the shore without longing for the certainties established on the artificial rock of our speculation.

Not theoretical speculation but the sense of the ineffable precipitates the problem of all problems. Not the apparent but the hidden in the apparent; not the wisdom but the mystery of the design of the universe; the questions we do not know how to ask have always poured oil on the flames of man's anxiety. Religion begins with the sense of the ineffable, with the awareness of a reality that discredits our wisdom, that shatters our concepts. It is, therefore, the ineffable with which we must begin, since otherwise there is no problem; and it is its perception to which we must return since otherwise no solution will be relevant.

FAITH IS NOT A PRODUCT of our will. It occurs without intention, without will. Words expire when uttered, and faith is like the silence that draws lovers near, like a breath that shares in the wind.

It is neither an inference from logical premises nor the outcome of a feeling that leads us to believe in His existence; it is not an idea gained by sitting back and observing or by going into the soul and listening to one's inner voice. We do not believe because we have come to a conclusion . . . or because we have been overcome by emotion. . . . It is a turning within the mind by a power from beyond the mind, a shock and collision with the unbelievable by which we are coerced into believing.

MEN HAVE OFTEN TRIED to give itemized accounts of why they must believe that God exists. Such accounts are like ripe wheat we harvest upon the surface of the earth. Yet it is beyond all reasons, beneath the ground, where a seed turns to be a tree, where the act of faith takes place.

The soul rarely knows how to raise its deeper secrets to discursive levels of the mind. We must not, therefore, equate the act of faith with its expression. The expression of faith is an affirmation of truth, a definite judgment, a conviction, while faith itself is an act, something that happens rather than something that is stored away; it is a moment in which the soul of man communes with the glory of God.

What is the nature of that act? How does it come about?

The question of the psalmist: "Is there a man of reason who seeks God?" (14:2) was interpreted by Rabbi Mendel of Kotzk to mean: Is a man who has nothing but his own reason capable of seeking God?

Many of us are willing to embark upon any adventure, except to go into stillness and to wait, to place all the wealth of wisdom in the secrecy of the soil, to sow our own soul for a seed in that tract of land allocated to every life which we call time – and to let the soul grow beyond itself. Faith is the fruit of a seed planted in the depth of a lifetime.

Many of us seem to think that faith is a convenient shortcut to the mystery of God across the endless, dizzy highway of critical speculation. The truth is that faith is not a way but the breaking of a way, of the soul's passageway constantly to be dug through mountains of callousness. Faith is neither a gift which we receive undeservedly nor a treasure to be found inadvertently.

We do not stumble into achievements. Faith is the fruit of hard, constant care and vigilance, of insistence upon remaining true to a vision; not an act of inertia but an aspiration to maintain our responsiveness to Him.

Just as people are unable to notice the most obvious phenomena in nature unless they are anxious to know about them – as no scientific insight will occur to those who are unprepared – so are they incapable of grasping the divine unless they grow sensitive to its supreme relevance. Without cleanliness of will the mind is impervious to the relevance of God. . . .

The art of awareness of God, the art of sensing His presence in our daily lives, cannot be learned off-hand. God's grace resounds in our lives like a staccato. Only by retaining the seemingly disconnected notes comes the ability to grasp the theme.

IN THE LIGHT OF FAITH we do not seek to unveil or to explain but to perceive and to absorb the rarities of mystery that shine out from all things; not to know more but to be attached to what is more than anything we can grasp. Only those who maintain that all things in life and death are within reach of their will try to place the world within the frame of their knowledge. But who can forever remain insensitive to the fragrance of the holy bestowed upon life?

With the gentle sense for the divine in all existence, for the sacred relevance of all being, the pious man can afford to forego the joy of knowing, the thrill of perceiving. He who loves the grandeur of what faith discloses dwells at a distance from his goal, eschews familiarity with what is necessarily hidden, and looks for neither proofs nor miracles. God's existence can never be tested by human thought. All proofs are mere demonstrations of our thirst for Him. Does the thirsty one need proof of his thirst?

The realm toward which faith is directed can be approached but not penetrated; approximated but not entered; aspired to but not grasped; sensed but not examined. For to have faith is to abide rationally outside, while spiritually within, the mystery.

Faith is an act of the spirit. The spirit can afford to acknowledge the superiority of the divine; it has the fortitude to realize the greatness of the transcendent, to love its superiority. The man of faith is not enticed by the ostensible. He abstains from intellectual arrogance and spurns the triumph of the merely obvious. He knows that possession of truth is devotion to it. Rejoicing more in giving than in acquiring, more in believing than in perceiving, he can afford to disregard the deficiencies of reason. This is the secret of the spirit, not disclosed to reason: the adaptation of the mind to what is sacred, intellectual humility in the presence of the supreme. The mind surrenders to the mystery of spirit, not in resignation but in love. Exposing its destiny to the ultimate, it enters into an intimate relationship with God.

Is it surrender to confide? Is it a sacrifice to believe? True, beliefs are not secured by demonstrations nor are they impregnable to objection. But does goodness mean serving only as long as rewarding lasts? Towers are more apt to be shaken than graves. Insistent doubt, contest, and frustration may stultify the trustworthy mind, may turn temples into shambles. Those of faith who plant sacred thoughts in the uplands of time – the secret gardeners of the Lord in mankind's desolate hopes – may slacken and tarry, but they rarely betray their vocation.

It is extremely easy to be cynical. It is as easy to deny His existence as it is to commit suicide. Yet no one is deprived of some measure of *suggestibility to the Holy*. Even the poorest souls have wings, soaring above where despair sees a ceiling.

IT IS NOT FROM EXPERIENCE but *from our inability to experience* what is given to our mind that certainty of the realness of God is derived. It is not the order of being but the transcendent in the contingency of all order, the allusions to transcendence in all acts and all things that challenge our deepest understanding.

Our certainty is the result of wonder and radical amazement, of awe before the mystery and meaning of the totality of life beyond our rational discerning. Faith is *the response* to the mystery, shot through with meaning; the response to a challenge which no one can forever ignore. "The heaven" is a challenge. When you "lift up your eyes on high," you are faced with the question. Faith is an act of man who *transcending himself* responds to Him who *transcends the world*.

Such response is a sign of man's essential dignity. For the essence and greatness of man do not lie in his ability to please his ego, to satisfy his needs, but rather in his ability to stand above his ego, to ignore his own needs; to sacrifice his own interests for the sake of the holy. The soul's urge to judge its own judgments, to look for meaning beyond the scope of the tangible and finite – in short, the soul's urge *to rise above its own wisdom* – is the root of religious faith.

God is the great mystery, but our faith in Him conveys to us more understanding of Him than either reason or perception is able to grasp.

Rabbi Mendel of Kotsk was told of a great saint who lived in his time and who claimed that during the seven days of the Feast of Booths his eyes would see Abraham, Isaac, Jacob, Joseph, Moses, Aaron, and David come to the booth. Said Rabbi Mendel: "I do not see the heavenly guests; I only have faith that they are present in the booth, and to have faith is greater than to see."

This, indeed, is the greatness of man: to be able to have faith. For faith is an act of freedom, of independence of our own limited faculties, whether of reason or sense-perception. It is *an act of spiritual ecstasy*, of rising above our own wisdom.

In this sense, the urge of faith is the reverse of the artistic act in which we try to capture the intangible in the tangible. In faith, we do not seek to decipher, to articulate in our own terms, but to rise above our own wisdom, to think of the world in the terms of God, to live in accord with what is relevant to God.

To have faith is not to capitulate but to rise to a higher plane of thinking. To have faith is not to defy human reason but rather to share divine wisdom.

"Lift up your eyes on high and see who created these" (Isa. 40:26). One must rise to a higher plane of thinking in order to see, in order to sense the allusions, the glory, the presence. One must rise to a higher plane of living and learn to sense the urgency of the ultimate question, the supreme relevance of eternity. He who has not arrived at the highest realm, the realm of the mystery; he who does not realize he is living at the edge of the mystery; he who has only a sense for the obvious and apparent, will not be able to lift up his eyes, for whatever is apparent is not attached to the highest realm; what is highest is hidden. Faith, believing in God, is attachment to the highest realm, the realm of the mystery. This is its essence. Our faith is capable of reaching the realm of the mystery.

UNLIKE SCIENTIFIC THINKING, understanding
for the realness of God does not come about by way
of syllogism, by a series of abstractions, by a thinking
that proceeds from concept to concept, but by way
of insights. The ultimate insight is the outcome of
moments when we are stirred beyond words, of instants
of wonder, awe, praise, fear, trembling, and radical
amazement; of awareness of grandeur, of perceptions we
can grasp but are unable to convey, of discoveries of the
unknown, of moments in which we abandon the pre-
tense of being acquainted with the world, of *knowledge
by inacquaintance.* It is at the climax of such moments
that we attain the certainty that life has meaning, that
time is more than evanescence, that beyond all being
there is someone who cares.

To repeat, it is only in such moments, in moments
lived on the level of the ineffable, that the categories and
acts of religion are adequately meaningful. Acts of love
are only meaningful to a person who is in love, and not to
him whose heart and mind are sour. The same applies to
the categories of religion. For ultimate insight takes place
on the presymbolic, preconceptual level of thinking. It
is difficult, indeed, to transpose insights phrased in the

presymbolic language of inner events into the symbolic language of concepts.

In conceptual thinking, what is clear and evident at one moment remains clear and evident at all other moments. Ultimate insights, on the other hand, are events, rather than a permanent state of mind; what is clear at one moment may subsequently be obscured. Concepts we acquire and retain. We have learned that two plus two equals four, and once we become convinced of the validity of this equation, the certainty will not leave us. In contrast, the life of the spirit is not always at its zenith, and the mercy of God does not at all times bestow upon man the supreme blessings.

MAN'S WALLED MIND has no access to a ladder upon which he can, on his own strength, rise to knowledge of God. Yet his soul is endowed with translucent windows that open to the beyond. And if he rises to reach out to Him, it is a reflection of the divine light in him that gives him the power for such yearning. We are at times ablaze against and beyond our own power, and unless man's soul is dismissed as an insane asylum, the spectrum analysis of that ray is evidence for the truth of his insight.

For God is not always silent, and man is not always blind. God's glory fills the world; His spirit hovers above the waters. There are moments in which, to use a Talmudic phrase, heaven and earth kiss each other; in which there is a lifting of the veil at the horizon of the known, opening a vision of what is eternal in time. Some of us have at least once experienced the momentous realness of God. Some of us have at least caught a glimpse of the beauty, peace, and power that flow through the souls of those who are devoted to Him. There may come a moment like a thunder in the soul, when man is not only aided, not only guided by God's mysterious hand, but also taught how to aid, how to guide other beings.

12

Not Our Vision of God but God's Vision of Us

OUR POINT OF DEPARTURE is not the sight of the shrouded and inscrutable; from the endless mist of the unknown we would, indeed, be unable to derive an understanding of the known. It is the tension of the known and the unknown, of the common and the holy, of the nimble and the ineffable, that fills the moments of our insights.

We do not owe our ultimate question to stumbling in a mist of ignorance upon a wall of inscrutable riddles. We do not ask because of our being poor in spirit and bereft of knowledge; we ask because we sense a spirit which surpasses our ability to comprehend it. We owe our question not to something less but to something which is more than the known. We ask because the world is too much for us, because the known is crammed with marvel, because the world is replete with what is more than the world as we understand it.

The question about God is not a question about all things, but a question of all things; not an inquiry into the unknown but an inquiry into that which all things stand for; a question we ask for all things. It is phrased not in categories of reason but in *acts* in which we are astir beyond words. The mind does not know how to phrase it, yet the soul sighs it, sings it, pleads it.

OUR AWARENESS OF GOD is a syntax of the silence, in which our souls mingle with the divine, in which the ineffable in us communes with the ineffable beyond us. It is the afterglow of years in which soul and sky are silent together, the outgrowth of accumulated certainty of the abundant, never-ebbing presence of the divine. All we ought to do is to let the insight be and to listen to the soul's recessed certainty of its being a parenthesis in the immense script of God's eternal speech.

The great insight is not attained when we ponder
or infer the beyond from the here. In the realm of the
ineffable, God is not a hypothesis derived from logical
assumptions, but an immediate insight, self-evident as
light. He is not something to be sought in the darkness
with the light of reason. In the face of the ineffable He
is the light. When the ultimate awareness comes, it is
like a flash, arriving all at once. To meditative minds the
ineffable is cryptic, inarticulate: dots, marks of secret
meaning, scattered hints, to be gathered, deciphered, and
formed into evidence; while in moments of insight the
ineffable is a metaphor in a forgotten mother tongue.

Thus, awareness of God does not come by degrees:
from timidity to intellectual temerity; from guesswork,
reluctance, to certainty; it is not a decision reached at
the crossroads of doubt. It comes when, drifting in the
wilderness, having gone astray, we suddenly behold the
immutable polar star. Out of endless anxiety, out of denial
and despair, the soul bursts out in speechless crying.

WHAT GIVES BIRTH to religion is not intellectual
curiosity, but the fact and experience of our being asked.
As long as we frame and ponder our own questions, we
do not even know how to ask. We know too little to be

able to inquire. Faith is not the product of search and endeavor, but the answer to a challenge which no one can forever ignore. It is ushered in not by a problem, but by an exclamation. Philosophy begins with man's question; *religion begins with God's question and man's answer.*

ACCUSTOMED TO THINKING in categories of space, we conceive of God as being vis-à-vis ourselves, as if we were here and He were there. We think of Him in the likeness of things, as if He were a thing among things, a being among beings.

Entering the meditation about the ultimate, we must rid ourselves of the intellectual habit of converting reality into an object of our minds. Thinking of God is totally different from thinking about all other matters; to apply the usual logical devices would be like trying to blow away a tempest with a breath. We often fail in trying to understand Him, not because we do not know how to extend our concepts far enough, but because we do not know how to begin close enough. To think of God is not to find Him as an object in our minds, but to find ourselves in Him. Religion begins where experience ends, and the end of experience is a perception of our being perceived.

To have knowledge of a thing is to have its concept at our mind's disposal. Since concept and thing, definition and essence belong to different realms, we are able to conquer and to own a thing theoretically, while the thing itself may be away from us, as is the case, for example, in our knowledge of stellar nebulae.

God is neither a thing nor an idea; He is within and beyond all things and all ideas. Thinking of God is not beyond but within Him. The thought of Him would not be in front of us, if God were not behind it.

The thought of God has no façade. We are all in it as soon as it is all in us. To conceive it is to be absorbed by it, like the present in the past, in a past that never dies.

Our knowing Him and His reality are not apart. To think of Him is to open our minds to His all-pervading presence, to our being replete with His presence. To think of things means to have a concept within the mind, while to think of Him is like walking under a canopy of thought, like being surrounded by thought. He remains beyond our reach as long as we do not know that our reach is within Him; that He is the Knower and we are the known; that to be means to be thought of by Him.

THE BIBLE IS PRIMARILY not man's vision of God but God's vision of man. The Bible is not man's theology but God's anthropology, dealing with man and what He asks of him rather than with the nature of God. God did not reveal to the prophets eternal mysteries but His knowledge and love of man. It was not the aspiration of Israel to know the Absolute but to ascertain what He asks of man; to commune with His will rather than with His essence.

In the depth of our trembling, all that we can utter is the awareness of our being known to God. Man cannot see God, but man can be seen by God. He is not the object of a discovery but the subject of revelation.

There are no concepts which we could appoint to designate the greatness of God or to represent Him to our minds. He is not a being, whose existence could be either confirmed or described by our thoughts. He is a reality, in the face of which, when becoming alive to its meaning, we are overtaken with a feeling of infinite unworthiness.

THE QUESTION BREAKS FORTH with the realization that it is man who is the problem; that more than God is a problem to man, man is a problem to God. The question: Is there a personal God? is a symptom of the uncertainty: Is there a personal man?

In moments in which the soul undergoes the unmitigated realization of the mystery that vibrates between its precarious existence and its inscrutable meaning, we find it unbearably absurd to define the essence of man by what he knows or by what he is able to bring about. To the sense of the ineffable the essence of man lies in his being a means of higher expression, in his being an intimation of ineffable meaning.

THE SENSE FOR THE REALNESS of God will not be found in insipid concepts; in opinions that are astute, arid, timid; in love that is scant, erratic. Sensitivity to God is given to a broken heart, to a mind that rises above its own wisdom. It is a sensitivity that bursts all abstractions. It is not a mere playing with a notion. There is no conviction without contrition; no affirmation without self-engagement. Consciousness of God is a response, and God is a challenge rather than a notion. We do not think Him, we are stirred by Him. We can never describe Him, we can only return to Him. We may address ourselves to Him; we cannot comprehend Him. We can sense His presence; we cannot grasp His essence.

His is the call, ours the paraphrase; His is the creation, ours a reflection. He is not an object to be comprehended, a thesis to be endorsed; neither the sum of all that is (facts) nor a digest of all that ought to be (ideals). He is the ultimate subject.

The trembling sense for the hereness of God is the assumption of our being accountable to Him. God-awareness is not an act of God being known to man; it is the awareness of man's being known by God. In thinking about Him we are thought by Him.

A HASID, IT IS TOLD, after listening to the discourse of one who lectured to him about the lofty concept of God according to the philosophers, said: "If God were the way you imagine Him, I would not believe in Him." However subtle and noble our concepts may be, as soon as they become descriptive, namely, definite, they confine Him and force Him into the triteness of our minds. Never is our mind so inadequate as in trying to describe God. The same applies to the idea of revelation. When defined, described, it completely eludes us.

THE QUESTION MAY BE ASKED: Is it plausible to believe that the eternal should be concerned with the trivial? Should we not rather assume that man is too insignificant to be an object for His concern? The truth, however, is that nothing is trivial. What seems infinitely small in our eyes is infinitely great in the eyes of the infinite God. Because the finite is never isolated; it is involved in countless ways in the course of infinite events. And the higher the level of spiritual awareness, the greater is the degree of sensibility to, and concern for, others.

We must continue to ask: What is man that God should care for him? And we must continue to remember that it is precisely God's care for man that constitutes the greatness of man. *To be* is to *stand for*, and what man stands for is the great mystery of being His partner. *God is in need of man.*

THIS IS WHAT WE MEAN by the term *spiritual*: It is the reference to the transcendent in our own existence, the direction of the Here toward the Beyond. It is the ecstatic force that stirs all our goals, redeeming values from the narrowness of being ends in themselves, turning arrivals into new pilgrimages, new farings forth. It is an all-pervading trend that both contains and transcends all values, a never-ending process, the upward movement of being. The spiritual is not something we own, but something we may share in. We do not possess it; we may be possessed by it. When we perceive it, it is as if our mind were gliding for a while with an eternal current, in which our ideas become knowledge swept beyond itself. It is impossible to grasp spirit in itself. Spirit is a *direction*, the turning of all beings to God.

TO THE PROPHET ... God does not reveal Himself in an abstract absoluteness, but in a personal and intimate relation to the world. He does not simply command and expect obedience; He is also moved and affected by what happens in the world, and reacts accordingly. Events and human actions arouse in Him joy or sorrow, pleasure or wrath. He is not conceived as judging the world in detachment. He reacts in an intimate and subjective manner, and thus determines the value of events. Quite obviously in the biblical view, man's deeds may move Him, affect Him, grieve Him or, on the other hand, gladden and please Him. This notion that God can be intimately affected, that He possesses not merely intelligence and will, but also pathos, basically defines the prophetic consciousness of God.

The God of the philosophers is like the Greek *anankē*, unknown and indifferent to man; He thinks, but does not speak; He is conscious of Himself, but oblivious to the world; while the God of Israel is a God who loves, a God who is known to, and concerned with, man. He not only rules the world in the majesty of His might and wisdom, but reacts intimately to the events of history. He does not judge people's deeds impassively and with aloofness; His judgment is imbued with the attitude of one to whom those actions are of the most intimate and profound concern. God does not stand outside the range of human suffering and sorrow. He is personally involved in, even stirred by, the conduct and fate of man.

Pathos denotes not an idea of goodness, but a living care; not an immutable example, but an outgoing challenge, a dynamic relation between God and man; not mere feeling or passive affection, but an act or attitude composed of various spiritual elements; no mere contemplative survey of the world, but a passionate summons.

THE BIBLE SPEAKS in the language of man. It deals with the problems of man, and its terms are borrowed from the vocabulary of the people. It has not coined many words, but it has given new meaning to borrowed words. The prophets had to use anthropomorphic language in order to convey His nonanthropomorphic Being.

The greatest challenge to the biblical language was how to reconcile in words the awareness of God's transcendence with His overwhelming livingness and concern. Had the biblical man recoiled from using anthropomorphic words, he never would have uttered: "The Lord is my shepherd, I shall not want." On the other hand, to assume that the psalmist, in using the word "shepherd," had the image of a shepherd in his mind is to misunderstand the meaning of that passage.

It is precisely the challenge involved in using inadequate words that drives the mind beyond all words. Any pretension to adequacy would be specious and a delusion.

To others, God seems to recede in a distance; to the prophets, He calls continually for participation. What the prophets experience, they demand of the people: not a fleeting experience of extraordinary surrender, but a perpetual attitude of obedience; not to stand "outside oneself," but to love Him with the whole self; not to lose one's destiny, but to remember one's destiny: being called, being chosen.

This was the central endeavor of the prophet: to set forth not only a divine law, but a divine life; not only a covenant, but also a pathos; not the eternal immutability of His Being, but the presence of His pathos in time; not only absolute Lordship, but also direct relatedness to man.

God is not a point at the horizon of the mind, but is like the air that surrounds one and by which one lives. He is not a thing, but a happening. The psalmist may ask man to meditate on God's works; the prophets call upon man to consider God's inner acts. They not only sense God in history, but also history in God.

All expressions of pathos are attempts to set forth God's aliveness. One must not forget that all our utterances about Him are woefully inadequate. But when taken to be allusions rather than descriptions, understatements rather than adequate accounts, they are aids in evoking our sense of His realness.

Notes

Reading Abraham Joshua Heschel Today

1. Every Moment Touches Eternity

2. The Only Life Worth Living

3. In the Presence of Mystery

4. The Prophets Show Us God Cares

5. God Demands Justice

6. Modernity Has Forfeited the Spirit

7. Prayer Is Being Known by God

8. A Pattern for Living

9. The Deed Is Wiser than the Heart

10. Something Is Asked of Us

11. Faith Is an Act of the Spirit

12. Not Our Vision of God but God's Vision of Us

Bibliography

Heschel, Abraham Joshua. *The Earth Is the Lord's: The Inner World of the Jew in East Europe*. New York: Henry Schuman, 1950.

_____. *God in Search of Man: A Philosophy of Judaism*. New York: The Noonday Press: Farrar, Straus and Giroux, 1955.

_____. *The Insecurity of Freedom: Essays on Human Existence*. New York: Farrar, Straus and Giroux, 1966.

_____. *Man Is Not Alone: A Philosophy of Religion*. New York: The Noonday Press: Farrar, Straus and Giroux, 1951.

_____. *Man's Quest for God: Studies in Prayer and Symbolism*. Santa Fe, New Mexico: Aurora Press, 1954.

_____. *The Prophets*. New York: Harper and Row, 1962.

_____. *The Sabbath*. New York: Farrar, Straus and Giroux, 1951.

_____. *Who Is Man?* Stanford, CA: Stanford University Press, 1965.

Heschel, Susannah. *Moral Grandeur and Spiritual Audacity: Essays of Abraham Joshua Heschel*. New York: Farrar, Straus and Giroux, 1996.

Plough Spiritual Guides

The Reckless Way of Love
Notes on Following Jesus
Dorothy Day

Love in the Void
Where God Finds Us
Simone Weil

The Prayer God Answers
Eberhard Arnold and Richard J. Foster

Why We Live in Community
Eberhard Arnold and Thomas Merton

The Scandal of Redemption
When God Liberates the Poor, Saves Sinners, and Heals Nations
Oscar Romero

That Way and No Other
Following God through Storm and Drought
Amy Carmichael

Plough Publishing House
845-572-3455 ✦ info@plough.com
PO BOX 398, Walden, NY 12586, USA
Robertsbridge, East Sussex TN32 5DR, UK
4188 Gwydir Highway, Elsmore, NSW 2360, Australia
www.plough.com